Cambridge Elements ≡

Elements in Creativity and Imagination
edited by
Anna Abraham
University of Georgia, USA

SLOW WONDER

Letters on Imagination and Education

Peter O'Connor
University of Auckland

Claudia Rozas Gómez
University of Auckland

CAMBRIDGE
UNIVERSITY PRESS

Shaftesbury Road, Cambridge CB2 8EA, United Kingdom

One Liberty Plaza, 20th Floor, New York, NY 10006, USA

477 Williamstown Road, Port Melbourne, VIC 3207, Australia

314–321, 3rd Floor, Plot 3, Splendor Forum, Jasola District Centre, New Delhi – 110025, India

103 Penang Road, #05–06/07, Visioncrest Commercial, Singapore 238467

Cambridge University Press is part of Cambridge University Press & Assessment, a department of the University of Cambridge.

We share the University's mission to contribute to society through the pursuit of education, learning and research at the highest international levels of excellence.

www.cambridge.org
Information on this title: www.cambridge.org/9781009124393

DOI: 10.1017/9781009128292

First published 2022

A catalogue record for this publication is available from the British Library.

ISBN 978-1-009-12439-3 Paperback
ISSN 2752-3950 (online)
ISSN 2752-3942 (print)

Slow Wonder

Letters on Imagination and Education

Elements in Creativity and Imagination

DOI: 10.1017/9781009128292
First published online: September 2022

Peter O'Connor
University of Auckland

Claudia Rozas Gómez
University of Auckland

Author for correspondence: Peter O'Connor, p.oconnor@auckland.ac.nz

Abstract: Slow wonder bears witness to the possibilities of the imagination. In a series of letters, the authors playfully imagine alternatives to current orthodoxies that privilege technocratic approaches to education and have strangled discussion about what it might mean to make education good and right, or even beautiful. The authors position the imagination as a powerful site of resistance within education and academic life. They unpack their philosophical positionings through vignettes of their teaching practice, poetry written as reflective musings and discursive theoretical pieces, including letters they have written to others. They attempt to marry the poetic and the academic, the rational and the affective, to model a slow approach to wondering about the joy, beauty and possibilities of life. In this spirit, they contemplate new ways to think and live in education.

Keywords: imagination, education, wonder, beauty, arts

ISBNs: 9781009124393 (PB), 9781009128292 (OC)
ISSNs: 2752-3950 (online), 2752-3942 (print)

Contents

1 Introduction

Slow wonder bears witness to the possibilities of the imagination. Our original commitment to this proposition started when we co-edited the book *Playing with Possibilities* in 2018.[1] In our introduction, we wrote:

> 'Imagination', as Emily Dickinson wrote, 'lights the slow fuse of possibility.'[2] Play and playing with possibilities [also] gives us something else the Romantics understood, the capacity to imagine and to slow wonder … The value of imagination, play and slow wonder, is connected to the idea that private imaginings are always connected to public possibilities … We unashamedly celebrate a romanticism which … represents a profound critique of some of modernity's most problematic and dehumanising features.

The book is a selection of the letters we have written to each other throughout 2021. The letters provided a searching dialogue for us to playfully imagine alternatives to current orthodoxies that privilege technocratic approaches to education and have strangled discussion about what it might mean to make education good and right, or even beautiful.

We position the imagination as a powerful site of resistance within education and academic life. The letters we write to each other unpack our philosophical positionings through vignettes of our teaching practice, poetry written as reflective musings and discursive theoretical pieces, including letters we have written to others. At the heart of the book, we include a series of letters where we contemplate a visit to an exhibition at the Auckland Art Gallery with the same title as this book. We send these letters to the curator of the exhibition, Julia Waite, who delights us by writing back. In our attempts to marry the poetic and the academic, the rational and the affective, we model a slow approach to wondering about the joy, beauty and possibilities of life. In this spirit, we contemplate new ways to think and live in education.

I have sent you the bones of my letters. Unwrap them carefully when you take them out of the box.

So my friend, these have rested unopened here all day. I'm going to open them tomorrow morning. I'll be careful with them. I'm excited. Talk tomorrow.

I sent you something. Read it! Read it!

---

[1] P. O'Connor & C. Rozas Gómez (eds), *Playing with Possibilities* (Cambridge: Cambridge Scholars Publishing, 2018).

[2] E. Dickinson, *The Poems of Emily Dickinson*, R. W. Franklin, ed., Reading Edition (Cambridge, MA: The Belknap Press of Harvard University Press, 1998).

I am having a family day tomorrow trying to dodge the virus while still having fun. Looking forward to our writing days next week and seeing the whole thing together in a sort-of book.

How many words?

I'm thinking more about what words.

2 Nailed to the Door

Claudia
Imagination

I put it on my door today. Before it goes up on my wall.

I like that.

I enjoyed putting it up. I stabbed it with a drawing pin.

In anger?

Compañero, it wasn't in anger.

What was it?

The stabbing? It was done with feeling, that's all.
I wasn't indifferent to the act.

But not anger?

No. Not anger, conviction.

I got into a rumble in a meeting today. It all started when I uttered a word that caused offence. I'm not sure who threw the first punch, but things got out of hand pretty quickly.

They said: it was too unclear, and not concrete enough, and how do you measure it, and it might even upset someone maybe someday.

I said: let's be wild and swim naked at midnight and maybe not know where the light falls and be stunned by everything.

But I could not convince anyone of my reason. To wonder – and wander. In the glimmer. So, I am thinking of having the word tattooed on my body or painted on my fence or fly it as a flag and make it my country, just as a reminder.

That I am not mad. Or that I did not commit a crime. Or that the moon has more than one phase.

For a while, I will have no other words, compañero.

Peter
Alchemy

Querida Claudia,

It feels so right to start our book with your Martin Luther moment. Who would have thought you could shake a system of belief to its very core by nailing questions to a door? Did you think your nailed poem in our shared corridor might upend the education monolith of sacred words and images, kick over the deity of evidence? Might we imagine a new, stripped down, more bare-footed way of walking inside classrooms?

It wasn't difficult for me to imagine your meeting. I've been in them too. Not exactly like that one, but the same confrontation and the same sense of nowhere to run. Needing to scream, to rumble. Twenty years ago, I was the National Facilitator for Drama for the New Zealand Ministry of Education. I was responsible for the teaching of drama in schools as the arts were made a compulsory part of the national curriculum. I sat in the dungeons of the Ministry of Education's building in Wellington with officials. We talked about learning in drama. Or, more accurately, I talked. Largely to myself. In my memory, it all took place on the equivalent of a film noir movie set in the 1950s. My arms handcuffed to the back of a chair in an interrogation cell in Moscow. It was nothing like this, because education bureaucrats are relentlessly amicable.

I remember saying, 'At the heart of all drama is play. That needs to front end the new curriculum.' There was that gentle but yet firm shaking of the head that I am sure is part of compulsory training for all government officials. 'Play. It's not really a word for a curriculum document', one scoffed. Another reprimanded, 'These are serious documents that people will critique, Peter. Curriculum documents are all about progression. Are you wanting children to develop skills in playing? Is that a legitimate role for schools?'

> 'But we make plays in drama and we make meaning by playing', I stuttered. 'Vygotsky, . . .'[3]
> 'Oh well, anyway' – that was the signal the conversation was over.

And there you were, trying it on again. Talking about things you know we're not supposed to talk about. What heretical musings on your part: mentioning the imagination in initial teacher education. Remember, words like imagination, play, joy, wonder and beauty – these are words that chill and confuse the education apparatchik. They aren't neat and tidy and predictable like dispositions and skills and plans and that list of other words I know you keep. The traitor words, the slippery eel words that trip lightly off the tongue of education researchers. The words with more than one side, but I'll leave you to write of those.

I give a lot of public lectures about the imagination. I start asking people to warm up their imaginations. To put their arms out in front of them and rub their hands together so they become hot and then I ask them to place them where they keep their imagination.

---

[3] L. S. Vygotsky, *Mind in Society: The Development of Higher Psychological Processes* (Cambridge, MA: Harvard University Press, 1978).

There are often nervous giggles, followed by furious rubbing and then pairs of hands fly. Often they land on the head. Maybe you can measure the imagination if its home is in the head, safely inside reason and thought. My friend Professor Kathy Stinear, a neuroscientist at the University of Auckland, says there is an enormous amount of neuro-bollocks written and spoken. She says it is often when people who are not trained in neuroscience but have read a little or googled a lot make outrageous claims about what the brain can or can't do. Neuroscientists know they cannot illuminate the soul or define meaning by scanning the brain. The biggest piece of neuro-bollocks I can think of is when non-scientists get overexcited by mirror neurons and then claim we have found where the imagination sits, as if it is simply a collection of tissues in the brain.

Science can never fully capture the magnificence or magical mystery of the imagination. If only Descartes, after weeks inside the oven, had come out and said, 'I imagine, therefore I am.' The bastard came out, sold out and doomed us to the dullness of logic and scientific rationalism. The head got privileged and we've never fully recovered. Antonio Damasio worked out that Spinoza should have won the debate,[4] so we might rightly understand that emotion and reason aren't enemies but instead are complementary essences of human existence. That the imagination and life itself are not some rational act that can be understood through observation of behaviour.

Others in the room put their warmed-up hands on their hearts. They see the imagination as an emotion, or perhaps a wave of emotions, something that sits inside their sense-based approach to the world. I realise sometimes that the imagination is a distinct place they go to. When the world is tipped upside-down, it is a refuge, a place of safety that is intensely and privately theirs. Perhaps, for some, the imagination provides a sense of freedom, a wistfulness of whimsy. It is possibly, in those moments, deliciously self-indulgent, like Belgian whole-cream chocolates. I wonder too, as I look at the room of people with hands planted on different parts of the body, why it's nearly always the men who touch their heads and the women who cover their hearts.

Others – children, and especially little ones – flutter their hands in the air and attempt to catch the imagination as formless fairy dust, only and barely visible to those who can still feel it in the air around them. I often try to remember what it felt like when I was little and I felt it land on me, when I could so easily scoop it up. My three-year-old granddaughter still grasps at pretend and play and invites me into her imagined worlds and I can't help but feel more alive. It's how I feel sometimes when I write while listening to Van Morrison telling me about the

4 A. R. Damasio, *Looking for Spinoza: Joy, Sorrow, and the Feeling Brain* (Boston: Houghton Mifflin Harcourt, 2003).

music in my soul and I'm reaching, reaching for the fabric softener of the imagination to wash across my words. The Romantics understood that the imagination was in the air around us, in nature, to be found through divine, slow and purposeful inspiration of breath. Our colleague was right, in an institution dedicated to measuring the individual, thank the gods you can't measure fairy dust.

I watched an older Māori woman, just the other night in a meeting, rub her hands and cover her eyes. When I asked what she was doing, she said her imagination comes through and also out of her eyes and it is in all her body. She said, 'It sits deeply inside me. It makes my legs dance, my lips sing, my hands touch and feel the world.' There was no one place where it sat; it was in and part of everything. She pointed to where Mount Taranaki, her ancestral mountain, stands, and said, 'And don't go thinking it is only us humans who have imagination.' Post-human Gnosticism perhaps?

At a public meeting on the state of the arts and creativity in New Zealand schools, a senior representative of the New Zealand Ministry of Education admonished my advocacy for the arts by saying I was making a mistake in assuming everyone is creative. She wondered out loud how many people even wanted to be creative. She said that, of her two grandchildren, one child was interested in engineering and the other one, who was 'quite creative' (a little girl, coincidentally), they sent to a Steiner school. She saw no need for schools to be places where little hands might be warmed, where children might be reminded of the power of fairy dust, or feel their imaginations in and through their bodies. I wanted to ask what had died inside her to make her think she lacked imagination, or why the slow fuse had never been lit. My heart went out to her. Later that night, I literally wept in cold despair. Now my heart goes out to our colleagues in your meeting who think the value of something is determined only by what can be measured.

In 2018, I worked with children in Mexico City just weeks after a deadly earthquake struck the city. We were busy making theatre about torn dream cloths and how they might be repaired. Many of the children warmed up their imagination by rubbing their stomachs. I wonder if they were seeing the imagination as instinctual, a gut-level response to the world. Perhaps they were showing it is something that feeds us and something that can be fed. My Spanish wasn't good enough to ask. Jung saw the imagination like these children did. He, thought, 'Every good idea and creative work owes its origination from the imagination and fantasy, with "play" acting as the dynamic principle, a key instinct, ranked alongside sex and nutrition.'[5]

---

[5] R. Matthews, 'An analytical psychology view on wholeness', *International Journal of Jungian Studies*, 7(2015), 124–38, 126.

Rubbing hands, warming things up. Ancient alchemists sought to turn ordinary metal into gold through friction, through the application of extreme heat on base metals. They searched for the philosopher's stone, sometimes also called 'the tincture' or 'the powder'. Perhaps what frightens so many about the imagination is that it might be no more than an invisible tincture with enormous power to bring about elemental change. Perhaps it is the essence of the magnus opus, the great work that ancient alchemists understood could heal the sick and transform the searcher into a perfect philosopher. We might then understand the imagination as the elixir of life, the powder that keeps us as wise as children, that makes us live beyond our death in the art we make. For the imagination lifts us out of the everyday and turns the greyness of life a golden hue. Is the imagination, then, the means by which we might achieve life's purpose, as Paolo Freire suggests, of becoming more fully human? James Hillman writes:

> We must start, as [the alchemist] Benedictus Figulus says, in the caelum, the sky-blue firmament over our heads, the mind already in the blue of heaven, imagination opened. The blue caelum of imagination gives to the opus a rock-hard standpoint from above downward, just as firm and solid as literal physical reality. A sapphire stone already at the beginning.[6]

Colega, I seem to have wandered a long way from your anguish about the imagination and its place in initial teacher education. And yet. And yet, perhaps not so far. For perhaps our colleagues and the Ministry of Education official also understand its limitations. Perhaps they recognise that tinctures and powders or philosopher's stones can't and shouldn't be measured. And, just perhaps, imagination should exist separately from the dark satanic mills of modern schooling.

And as I write about alchemy and heat, I remember how and why I became a drama teacher. It's a story I've told elsewhere,[7] and I have a feeling I might return to it later. It's when I joined a rebel church outside the orthodoxy. The big booming church of radical pedagogy: arts inspired us and drama was our communion.

In 1979, as my undergraduate university days drew to a close and the thoughts of writing and politics swirled in my head, a good friend of mine invited me to a recruitment evening for teacher training. Dave assured me that the evening also had free wine and cheese. We sat down and someone said they were going to show a reel-to-reel film[8] showcasing the drama work of Dorothy Heathcote, who had been out to New Zealand the year before. It was supposed

---

[6] J. Hillman, 'Alchemical blue and the unio mentalis', *Sulfur* 1 (1981), 1–11, 7.

[7] P. O'Connor, *Pedagogy of Surprise* (Sydney: Drama Australia, 2015).

[8] J. Neher, *Three Looms Waiting* (Time-Life Films, 1974).

to show what was now possible in schools. I was mesmerised by her teaching. I had never seen anything like it before, and the real direction and purpose of the rest of my life unfolded at that moment.

I remember in particular the smile of a young boy. He was part of a group working with Dorothy's master's students in a school for children with disabilities. The children pulled Dorothy's students across the floor and piled them in a great twisted heap: a bonfire waiting to be set alight. In a moment of pure dramatic magic, the little boy stood before one teacher who was to be set alight. He held out his empty hands and told the teacher not to worry: 'See, they're pretend matches.' He knew the pretend match in his hand couldn't hurt the piled-up bodies on the floor. He grabbed the hands of the teacher and headed towards the pile with glee, with joy, totally absorbed in the task and yet revelling in the pretence. I immediately saw the work as deeply political. It was poetry in action, poetry of movement, of gesture, of defiance, of resistance. In that moment, I became a drama teacher for the rest of my life. It was a road to Damascus conversion. For I began to understand, as Plutarch did, that I might work with children and young people to light fires, rather than fill pails:

> For this knowledge is not something that can be put into words like other sciences; but after long-continued dialogue between teacher and pupil, in joint pursuit of the subject, suddenly, like light flashing forth when a fire is kindled, it is born in the soul and straightway nourishes itself.[9]

I wanted to realise teaching as poetry in motion: teaching as alchemy, teaching as magical pretence, teaching that used the crucible of the arts to create whole imagined worlds. Alchemical teaching that transformed teacher and student. The magnus opus of my life has been to refine my skills and understandings of my personal tinctures and powders so I might conjure gold in classrooms. It's a never-ending journey, but I know that imagination, joy and wonder are the ephemeral, immeasurable elements of my crucible.

Claudia
Leaving Church

Dear Peter,

I am trying to unravel how everything started to unravel. To pinpoint the moment when the orthodoxy grew tentacles and wrapped itself around all that we do. At what point did 'imagination' become a dangerous word in education? At what point did a bureaucrat decide that not all children are creative?

---

[9] Plutarch, *Plutarch's Lives: Translated from the Original Greek, with Notes, Critical and Historical, and a Life of Plutarch* (London: Derby & Jackson, 1859).

Perhaps the unravelling has been more like a slow smothering. All this time we have been breathing in without realising it was getting harder to breathe out.

Smothered is how I feel when I come out of that meeting. The proposal to develop students' educational imaginations as a course outcome has been rejected. My colleague and I are told the outcome is not clear enough, that students might find the notion confusing and potentially complain about the lack of clarity. In so many ways, my response feels disproportionate to the offence. My colleagues are not my enemies. But something about this meeting unsettles me and leaves me wondering how we got to this state of limp and lifeless edu-speak. The idea that students querying an outcome or seeking further clarification is something to be avoided is also disconcerting. Biesta would argue that risk is a fundamental aspect of pedagogy,[10] and yet the concern over student confusion suggests our job is to protect students from all levels of discomfort. I grab my phone and text a close friend.

'I almost got into a rumble for using the word "imagination".'

My friend is a writer, so his reaction is swift and merciless.

'Time for a revolution.'

Talk of insurgency doesn't feel like an overreaction on this afternoon, and I slowly rewrite my text on a piece of paper. I keep writing and my grievance turns into a declaration that I decide to place on my office door. I secure the writing with a drawing pin and commit to imagination and all the other old-world words that no one seems to use anymore. My Martin Luther moment is turning into something deeper.

To distract myself from the internal shaking, I turn to my collection of teas for consolation, but I am not long through a hot drink before an email pings on my screen. Microsoft is providing me with an 'in-depth view of my work patterns for the last four weeks'. The information provided is vast. For a start, it identifies my 'collaborators' – the people I email the most – and then ranks them like some strange popularity contest. Every month I wonder who will top my list and who will be voted off *Email Survivor*. The spying software also tells me how quickly I respond to emails – apparently, I respond to most within an hour. Sometimes, Microsoft thinks I have free time 'to focus' when I don't, but today it is chastising me for the hours I keep.

> You compromised your nightly recharge on 10 days last month by working past midnight. Ensure optimal nightly recharge by protecting the golden sleep time period (12am–5am) from work related activities.

---

[10] G. Biesta, *The Beautiful Risk of Education* (Abington: Routledge, 2015).

Golden sleep is only five hours long? The shaking returns. I would love more sleep. My family would probably love me more if I *had* more sleep. But the relentless list of administrative tasks we are meant to do and roles we are meant to inhabit get in the way of my 'nightly recharge'.

Our academic life is more about compliance than teaching and research these days; or rather, the compliance imperative governs our teaching and research in particular ways. The technologies (literal as well as in the Foucauldian sense) used to monitor our compliance come in the form of software that I never learn to use. In part, I don't learn because I am at war with the ideology of it all, and not engaging seems like a reasonable form of rebellion. But I also don't engage because of the time involved. There is always a workshop and a YouTube clip, and notes or a link to follow, and someone to email for further assistance. If the software requires this level of attention, then surely technology is a hindrance rather than a help.

A case in point is our annual performance review, which I haven't completed properly for the last three years. Consequently, every year I get the message that I have achieved 0 per cent of my goals. Given the online nature of the review, it is difficult to imagine that others are not privy to my reckless failure. Yet even such public exposure does little to motivate action on my behalf and I can see only two ways forward. The first is to stop having goals and to stop trying to improve myself. The other is to have radical, unmeasurable goals such as 'have humane relationships with my students' or 'be surprised by something' or 'find joy in a piece of writing'. (I have decided on the latter but keep the goals to myself.)

It is not just the administrative aspects of our work that smother us; it is also the ways in which our teaching is governed and shaped by policy. Our colleague, Barbara Grant, has written about this teaching context as the 'policification of university teaching'.[11] She talks about the way policy 'forces itself'[12] on teaching so we have no choice but to engage and construct ourselves in particular ways. After looking at the word 'policification' a second time, I realise it contains the words policy and police/policing in its possibilities for meaning. The play on the word is intentionally unforgiving, and Barbara's use of the word 'force' draws attention to the strangling nature of the impositions. As Barbara points out, the purpose of policy is to dominate teaching.[13] Although this policy is always presented as enhancing the way we work, policies are also ways of both managing what we do and ensuring student (customer) satisfaction.

---

[11] B. M. Grant, 'Becoming-teacher as (in)activist: Feeling and refusing the force of university policy', *Policy Futures in Education*, 19(5) (2021), 539–53, 543.
[12] Ibid., 540.   [13] Ibid.

Barbara suggests policy refusal as a form of resistance. I like the idea that my war with the ideology may involve laying down my sword and drinking tea instead. I look down at my current list of jobs and think about the ones I could refuse to complete. Too many of them are related to admin and policy compliance: write digital course outlines / write course reviews / update Talis / remind students to complete SET evaluations / complete my APR / familiarise myself with the assignment extension policy / place the official university banner on my Canvas course / complete the new CDDC form / update our Discovery Profiles. And so it goes.

Upon reflection, I can trace the journey of how we got here all the way back to my days as a first-year teacher. Or at least that's when this version of teaching started for me. I was formed as a teacher in the late 1990s when outcomes-based education prevailed. Outcomes needed to be observable and measurable, so the language we used when planning units of work was carefully constructed. We engaged in earnest backwards planning and never questioned its legitimacy. Planning from the outcome was a powerful practice because it identified us as good and competent teachers. Yet planning this way also meant I rarely asked questions about curriculum content. My focus was captured primarily by the outcome I was pursuing rather than what content might be worthy in a secondary English programme. Despite my socially radical reasons for becoming a teacher in the first place, my sense of professionalism was tied to the idea that I could execute teaching in watertight ways – a technocratic view of teaching intensified by the accompanying visibility of my students' results.

It seems to me that our troubles with imagination and its potentially diminished space within education are connected to the same rationalities that shape our academic lives: the idea that both education and our working lives can be organised around predetermined outcomes for narrow and finite purposes. I don't think we can blame the neuroscientists or Descartes. Maybe one day they *will* find the piece of brain or the exact neurons where the imagination lives. And thinking must surely involve the imagination. Our foe is the managerialist discourse that stems from our political economy. In submitting public service to businesslike models, our work is surrendered to customer satisfaction and the surveillance required to ensure we are always focused on being the right type of workers. Within this rationality, it follows that imagination is constituted as a risk. If invoking the imagination muddies the water in any way at all, it becomes an obstruction to education, rather than a possibility.

When I was in my final two years of high school, I was desperate to go to university. The desperation was so intense I would have vivid daydreams and night dreams about my imagined Shangri-La. One morning, I woke from a dream in which I saw myself walking along Barracks Wall behind the Old Choral Hall.

As I walked, I encountered different groups of people, each engaged in an action related to their field of study. Some groups were conducting experiments, others were engaged in performance, some were quietly writing, while others were immersed in a discussion. This non-cryptic dream is the version of university and the purpose of education that I imagined then and wish for now. Reflecting on this dream, I realise that my sense of the university was connected to a desire for self-actualisation. It wasn't just about what I wished to study, but how I wished to move in the world. My 18-year-old sense of what this life would entail was fairly simplistic. I imagined watching arthouse films and discussing politics with like-minded people. This version of me implied a commitment to a thinking-life, and this version of education still prevails in my imagined landscapes within academia. Peter, I am still a believer.

We come to education with faith – we have to: belief is our primary qualification. We rise early and willingly to do our work because we believe in modernity's promise that education can make life better. Yet it is becoming difficult to wear the robes and utter the prayers, not because there is a lack of belief but because belief has been replaced with certainty. I once read that there is a difference between knowing and believing, that when we start knowing with too much certainty, we wander into the danger zone of dogma. So how to hold onto belief and let go of knowing in education?

Some time ago, when I was asked to explain my journey in education, I thought about the influence sociology had on my thinking. It occurred to me that sociology of education is like taking a pan shot, a disciplinary lens that captures the shifting landscape between education and society. In my explanation, I drew a distinction between knowing and seeing. I suggested that my travels through education had been a process of knowing less but seeing more. It is not surprising that C. Wright Mills refers to sociological thinking as the sociological *imagination*.[14] Perhaps he was summoning the Romantic poets and the 'inner eye' when he called on us to 'lucidly' interpret our place in society and society's place in us. Afterall, the Romantic poets used the notion of imagination as a means to question enlightenment ideals and the effects of the Industrial Revolution: they nailed imagination to the door.

The ability to see more and in new ways is joyful and sustaining; I would like more of that joy. I imagine a different type of academy and wonder what our joys would be if we were released from this neo-liberal, managerialist realism. I think also about the declaration on my office door and worry about the futility

---

[14] C. Wright Mills, *The Sociological Imagination* (Oxford; New York: Oxford University Press, 1959).

of its presence. If policy refusal is a form of resistance, what is the purpose of a hastily worded and emotionally charged disputation? Katie Barclay might see the words on my door as a performance of emotion,[15] one that offers a counterpoint to the ethics and norms of our institution. Nailing something to the door will always be a political act – a refusal of identity and an open challenge to current wisdom.

In the spirit of refusal and the performance of emotion, we need a new gospel. A reformation of sorts. We need new versions of academic life and new versions of a life in education where we can move and breathe freely. This conversation between us might be a good place to start; these pages seem like a good place to whisper and pray – and imagine.

Let's rub our hands together. Let's summon our inner eye and see what happens.

Peter
A Professional Creed

Dear Claudia,

I've already told you some of the story of how I became a teacher. It was a serendipitous outing with wine and cheese and Dorothy. It was a decade before you entered the church/profession. It was a very different time, before the neo-liberal revolution in New Zealand where we copied the nonsense of your homeland and manacled ourselves to the market. When literally a chain super-market merchant was tasked with reviewing and upending education. He created the monster we still live with forty years later. Without a trace of Orwellian irony, the ghastly experiment is still called 'Tomorrow's Schools', where each school has become a competing business unit. Winner and loser schools, focused on the narrowest of learning leading to standardised and thoroughly tested students, neatly packaged products for sale on the supermarket shelf of life.

I was blessed to sign on at a time when my early teaching pedagogy was shaped by key thinkers in drama education, such as Dorothy Heathcote, Gavin Bolton and David Booth. I read *Pedagogy of the Oppressed*[16] one afternoon in a bathtub with a bottle of cheap red wine, and was changed forever. Conscientised and drunk simultaneously. I realised that the drama teaching I was doing was part of a wider political and pedagogical tradition that embraced the work of bell hooks, Peter McLaren, Henri Giroux, Neil Postman, Bill Ayers.

And of course I became besotted with John Dewey. Seriously, how could you not? Education and democracy, education and the arts. Education is life itself,

---

[15] K. Barclay, *Academic Emotions: Feeling the institution* (Cambridge; New York: Cambridge Elements, 2021).

[16] P. Freire, *Pedagogy of the Oppressed* (Meersburg: Herder and Herder, 1972).

not a preparation for life.[17] His laboratory schools were alchemical. And he too believed in belief. In 1897 perhaps it was easier for him to write about his belief,[18] a personal and professional creed, rather than having to rely on meta this and meta that data, on meta synthesis and best evidence. He knew to value invisible rather than visible learning.[19]

In this book, perhaps we are following his tradition in declaring what we believe about education rather than what we know:

I believe in the idea that education is the intergenerational promise that we don't have to die in the same world we were born into.
I believe in the sacred responsibility of genuinely loving and caring for the children we teach.
I believe in the pursuit of beauty, joy and wonder in classrooms.
I believe beauty is a truth.
I believe despite the evidence, not because of it.
I believe in . . .
I believe in star dust on rocks in the Antarctic.
I believe in teaching as an improvisational art form.
I believe in a pedagogy of surprise.
I believe in invisible learning.
I believe in the Angelus.
I believe in egg sandwiches.
We believe we can fly.
I believe you can cross the sky.

Claudia, my teaching journey has been about doubting the new orthodoxies that have crowded out these beliefs that drew me into teaching and that sustain me now. As I flick through my back pages, I can't help but think I was so much older then. I'm younger than that now.

3 Slow Wonder

Peter
Slow Light – A Day at the Gallery

Claudia, when I started working at the university, I imagined that there would be many days like today.

I was your age when I started life as a full-time academic. Fifty. Before then I'd crafted a living making theatre, writing, teaching, travelling the world. I'd got a PhD in using theatre to counter stigma associated with mental illness and I was running a theatre in education programme on stopping family violence. I did short-term gigs making and researching theatre. A friend half-mockingly

---

[17] J. Dewey, *The Arts and Education* (London: Routledge, 1917).

[18] J. Dewey, *My Pedagogic Creed* (London: Routledge, 1897).

[19] J. Hattie, *Visible Learning* (Abingdon; New York: Routledge, 2008).

described me as a suitcase-academic peddling the arts as a panacea for the world's agonies. I remember those early years back in the university for the first time in nearly thirty years. I'd completed my PhD through distance, so I hadn't physically been full-time in a university since I finished my BA when I was only twenty.

I felt totally and completely alienated by this alternative world dedicated to counting things, where people were seemingly only motivated by an over-whelming desire, if not a nagging neediness, for promotion, the life-strangling hierarchy and everyone endlessly busy with a bureaucracy that even Kafka would have thought too strange for fiction. Perhaps I had imagined it would be like joining a monastic order where people contemplated the world. People who thought deep and meaningful things, heads in the clouds, removed from the world. I imagined I would sit with people and talk about big things, or simply take companionable walks. There'd be time to think, to finally write the things that had sat deep inside me for so long. And the time to read, to spend hours lost in other people's words and stories and dreams and hopes. My dad had left school when he was only twelve and I was the only one of my family of nine to go to university. I remember how much I had loved the Romantic poets in my undergraduate studies, but I felt completely lost in a sea of entitlement and money. So going to work in a university more than slightly terrified me. I had no idea then that faculty was just another word for factory. I had worked so hard to avoid the factory line on which I now found myself. One with privilege and money and access to long holidays and international travel pre Covid-19, so let's not indulge in a pity call about the academic life.

Today was a good day, a great day. Because it wasn't like most days in the university. There were the long slow conversations with you as we wandered in the art gallery. It reminded me of what is possible as an academic. The possibility of inspiration, to breathe in the art we witnessed and, like Wordsworth, maybe produce some writing akin to his understanding of poetry as

> the spontaneous overflow of powerful feelings: it takes its origin from emotion recollected in tranquillity: the emotion is contemplated till, by a species of reaction, the tranquillity gradually disappears, and an emotion, kindred to that which was before the subject of contemplation, is gradually produced, and does itself actually exist in the mind.[20]

I had hoped the university might be a place of quiet contemplation, a tranquil and unhurried place to recollect the work I had done for years, hawking my medicine of theatre and dance and music for a sick and tired world. I had hoped I might catch again the passion of the revolution in my words. I had hoped to

---

[20] W. Wordsworth, 'Preface to the lyrical ballads', *Arts Education Policy Review*, 105(2) (2003), 33–6.

disrupt the comfortable, and comfort those whose lives were disrupted by the greed of global capital.

Today reminded me that the full wonder and promise of an academic life is still possible when one deliberately privileges the time to notice the beauty of the world and finds time to frame a response to it. I grasped the privilege of being paid to think and write.

Perhaps I'm being overly dramatic – it was, after all, merely a trip to the art gallery to see the exhibition of New Zealand artist Bill Culbert. Perhaps my memory is coloured by it literally having been my last trip out into the world before Covid-19 threw us into a months-long strict lockdown. It was the last swim before the end of summer. The last lick of the melting ice-cream. My memory has been sharpened by the sudden and huge change to our world within hours of our visit. Covid lockdowns slow the world down, distort time, disturb any sense of meaning beyond the moment and force us into further isolation from colleagues and friends.

Yet, as I wrote this, I stopped to speak to a friend on the phone as she told me of the machinations behind decisions that might or might not impact my research work. As I listened to her, I was reminded of the brief visitor from Porlock interrupting the flow in caverns measureless to man. I said I was writing about writing in the academy. Her own sense of despair erupted.

'Remember', she said, 'those days when we could in a morning read, simply read and connect to the ideas that had determined our lives? Those days when we might give a lecture without notes and PowerPoints and every other digitised technology imaginable? Given playfully to students who barely took any notes because they could cram for exams and spend their time on campus falling in love and dreaming of revolution and falling out of love and lying in the sun in the park? One book every now and then, a good one laboured over with love, not rushed out as a research outcome? Remember those times when we could have long, rather meaningless but deeply important conversations in common rooms?'

I said I didn't remember. 'I started too late and now these things that to you seem to be at the heart of things are like stolen and forbidden fruits.' She muttered something about neo-liberalism and, although I agreed, I thought again that neo-liberalism is just a symptom of a deeper and more sinister cancer: a speeding up of the world that robs us of life.

Spilling light with you in the gallery reminded me of how the university might become more fully human. That old Freirean notion never strays too far from my thinking: 'How might education make humans more fully human?'[21] How might I claim my humanity inside the academy? As we sat in the café

---

[21] Freire, *Pedagogy of the Oppressed*.

determined to write differently, to think differently, to feel the power of our visit among the art, I found myself resistant to the need to produce yet another research output, stamped out by the machine. I imagined our book in this series, titled *Easy and Effective Strategies for Creative Classrooms: Innovative and Efficient Approaches to Standardised Assessment.* I felt queasy. Introduction. Research method. Literature review. Findings, limitations, recommendations and conclusion.

Neat, tidy, linear and ultimately self-serving. When you go online to record your research in the factory database, you click on the tab that says 'Research output'. You label and tidy it, then it gets counted alongside everything else you've done and then every six years it all gets counted as a bundled lot and then you get a number that records your value as an academic in relation to all the others who have done the very same thing. The rise of managerialism in the university was always designed to constrain the manner in which we work. We have been forced to work alone, polishing immaculate prose, arriving at definitions and conclusions, busy, busy, busy justifying our existence against the standard.

Today though we gave ourselves permission to
Write this one small book, re-collect the feelings we had
Enough of counting of the
circumscribed, circumspect and circumcised numbers
Attached to products.
ERICed
Today we wandered
You and I
We smiled at some of the same things
I wondered if you too were thinking
About spilt light
And the wine held tightly in the glass
where the light was tricked or the light tricked
me into looking far longer
than I look at the everyday

We took a photo of ourselves outside the exhibit.
Before we left
I'm not sure why
Photos of us sit on my phone.
Maybe at the book launch
We might look at them
And smile.

We had to go to the gallery. We called it research fieldwork. The exhibition was called *Slow Wonder* and the curator, Julia Waite, had named the exhibition after a conversation we had on a lazy summer's day in the Centre.

Julia had come to visit me because of my interest in the revolutionary arts movement in New Zealand, of which Culbert's teacher at high school, James Coe, had been a leading proponent. Talking of James Coe also led us to talk of other artist educators and the extraordinary gift of the spectacular blaze of colour in New Zealand schools that happened in the 1950s and 1960s. We spoke of Elwyn Richardson too, for in the corner of our seminar room in the Centre we have a display of sculptures and pots children had made in his school in the 1950s. People from around the world come and visit and marvel at them and the simplicity of his approach to learning. The porous walls of his classroom in the remote far north of New Zealand meant that children saw themselves in the liminal space between scientist and artist, deciphering the meaning of their local landscape by using it to make art with its mud and whatever else they could find. In the artworks you can tell their learning was an organic lived experience fuelled by a genuine love for the world. As we looked at the small gallery, I mentioned Maxine Greene and said that to me this work was the practical lived representation of her philosophy. We shared our thoughts about how Maxine understood the role of the gallery in educating children:

> to embark on a new beginning for oneself, a beginning generated by questioning, curiosity, wonder, restiveness [. . .] to understand the importance of uncoupling from the ordinary when entering the gallery, of trying to bracket out conventional seeing and expectation for a while.[22]

I said that perhaps we should understand the possibility of the gallery as a classroom and the classroom as gallery, where we might again wonder slowly, look deeply so we might see the brush strokes that shape our realities. I wondered too whether, in the days when the woke generation speaks to a consciousness of those who hold the brushes, Maxine Greene understood that schooling must be 'to awaken persons to a sense of present-ness, to a critical consciousness of what is ordinarily obscured'.[23]

Much of current living anaesthetises us, numbs us, so we are unable to perceive it as it is or sense a capacity to act on it. The opposite is *aesthetic* awareness, a door to wonderment waking us up to the beauty and joy of living. As Proust says, 'The real voyage of discovery consists not in seeking new landscapes but in having new eyes.'[24] The children's joy-filled pottery in the corner reminded us that the power of teaching centres on perceptions about how we might see the world afresh each time we see it.

---

[22] M. Greene, 'The art of being present: Educating for aesthetic encounters', *The Journal of Education*, 166(2) (1984), 123–35, 132.

[23] Ibid., 132.   [24] M. Proust, 'A la recherche du temps perdu', *La Prisonnière*, 6(2) (1923).

Our conversation slid into phenomenology, and Maurice Merleau-Ponty, and the relationship between perception and cognition. The perfect French philosopher's name. These lines of his have always spoken a truth to me:

> My field of perception is constantly filled with a play of colours, noises and fleeting tactile sensations which I cannot relate precisely to the context of my clearly perceived world, yet which I nevertheless immediately 'place' in the world, without ever confusing them with my daydreams. Equally constantly, I weave dreams round things. I imagine people and things whose presence is not incompatible with the context, yet who are not in fact involved in it: they are ahead of reality, in the realm of the imaginary.[25]

He speaks of weaving dreams round things when he also writes elsewhere of 'how the world's appearance would be shaken if we succeeded in perceiving the spaces in between things as things themselves'.[26] It is like poetry really, isn't it? The spaces between words are just silent or invisible words, but they are words nonetheless. Non-word words. And perhaps the imagination sits in these in-between places, between light and dark, between head and heart, between thought and action, between the past and the present, the living and the dead, and, in Merleau-Ponty's terms, between the visible and the invisible.

I told Julia about our book, *Playing with Possibilities*, and our introduction and how we wrote – or, perhaps more accurately, you wrote:

> At a time when it is common to have multiple tabs open on our screens and information is only a click away, the capacity to slow wonder should be fostered.

Julia's long fingers reached across the table and scrawled in her notebook:

> *Slow*
> *Wonder*

I told her we were writing a book about what slow wonder might look like, and over the course of the year as we wrote this book, Julia was creating her exhibition called *Slow Wonder* in the Auckland Art Gallery. It seems these ideas, of how we might reimagine the world, weave dreams in the space between light and dark through the shadows, how we might notice in the everyday the extraordinary lightness of living, was something that Bill Culbert had played with for years and that Julia too was playing with. We have toyed with the words and the non-words in this book and Julia arranged the objects into a space where people were encouraged to look and look again.

---

[25] M. Merleau-Ponty, *The Phenomenology of Perception* (London: Routledge, 2012[1945]), pp. xi, 37.

[26] M. Merleau-Ponty, *The Visible and the Invisible: Followed by Working Notes* (Evanstown, IL: Northwestern University Press, 1968).

On days like this, I find myself wondering if classrooms and galleries are unknown remembered gates that take us back to where we started.

Is that what classrooms and galleries are: remembered gates that take us back to where we started?

So today we went and saw what Julia had made of Bill Culbert.

I smiled deep into myself when we walked into the first exhibit, an extraordinary camera obscura, and your first words were, 'This reminds me of Maxine Green, the capacity to make the familiar strange.' I hadn't told you then of my conversation with Julia. I had guessed that your perception of the world hadn't been dulled by too many years in the university. I thought of the anaesthetic of the post-normal world where we become strangers to ourselves.

I wonder now too that if a classroom can be a gallery, we might see it as a place where it might disrupt our senses, so as 'to see the familiar made strange and the strange familiar'.

We looked at Culbert's fascination with light and the space in between:

Why is it always the space

in

be

tween?

The liminal

The liminal servants[27] as Peter McLaren would call us

Catholic liberation theology lapping against radical pedagogy

Washing feet

A pedagogy of love

The servant leader

The possibilities of existing between light and shadow

The interplay of light and shade

We stared at the wine glasses

Julia joined us in the gallery.

'I imagined you were at the end', she smiled, as she realised we had only moved fifty metres in an hour.

We are slow wondering, we laughed.

And Neruda came in a rush:

We need to sit on the rim

of the well of darkness

and fish for fallen light

with patience.

---

[27] P. L. McLaren, 'The liminal servant and the ritual roots of critical pedagogy', *Language Arts*, 65(2) (1988), 164–80.

I was going to tie this letter together, make some point about the limitations of the experience and what might have been learnt from it. I resisted. I stopped here – in the first room of the exhibit.

Claudia
Slow Light and Loose Arrangements

Peter . . . Peter . . . Peter . . .
Today we wandered

two friends and colleagues

You and I

fully fledged academics since we were 50

We smiled at some of the same things

finding delight

I wondered if you too were thinking

and marvelling

About spilt light

in silence

And the wine held tightly in the glass

taking communion

where the light was tricked, or the light tricked

a faithful surrender from you, and

me into looking far longer

for the first time, in a long time

than I look at the everyday

trapping light in our praying hands.

We took a photo of ourselves outside the exhibit.

By the sign with our book title

Before we left

we stepped back into our fast lives

I'm not sure why

we run like this

My photos sit on my phone.

wanting to escape,

Maybe at the book launch

when what we need is to slow down

We might look at them

for a moment – or maybe forever.

And smile.

As Slow as Light

I am the same age as you were when I become a fully fledged academic. Fifty. The journey to get here has been slow. On purpose and not. I wanted to be involved in the details of my child's life, so I chose the slower, steeper path. But there have been other things too. One is the university institution you refer to, and the ways in which it has become a meaner, more punishing machine. So punishing, in fact, that we end up asking questions about whether or not the academy can even be a humane place to work. After a morning of genuine contemplation, we are left wondering how we might create more days like this.

I like your idea of the university as a monastery; I suppose that's what monasteries were in the first instance. Places of slow and quiet learning. An unhurried existence is appealing to me; nothing spooks me like the demand for fast thought or action. My grandfather would say of us slowpokes that before we were able to move, one leg would have to ask the other leg for permission. The description is fitting for me, except that it is not just my legs, but my arms and my brain, and the nuclei in my cells too. Slowness is built into me. Yet academic life races through the fast lane. The fast university is a place of speedy production and consumption. Snooze and you lose. Perform or perish. As an alternative, the slow movement argues for slow scholarship, an affirmation of slowed down, reflective work. Against the performativity that fosters individualism and competition, slow scholarship is a form of resistance – like policy refusal. We could start by replacing our university's meritocratic motto from *Ingenio et Labore* to *Largo e Pianissimo*.

We think of light as the speediest traveller in the universe, but light can be slow when it is refracted through water or glass or diamond. Light is also slow in the form of sunlight that sneaks from one side of the house to the other throughout the course of the day. Our work should be as slow as that light.

The Shortest Distance between Two Points Is Light

Bill Culbert spent his life paying attention to light. His sustained observation is on display at the *Slow Wonder* exhibition at the Auckland Art Gallery – Toi O Tāmaki, where we meet on Tuesday, 17 August 2021 at 10 a.m. It feels important to record the date because this is the day Covid-19 properly caught up with our country, about eighteen months after the rest of the world. Slowness is built into New Zealand too. We meet for a reflective wander to see whether the exhibition, which shares the name of our book, leads to thought and writing over a shared lunch. We don't know it at the time, but this is the last day we will enjoy our Level 1 freedoms for the foreseeable future. It is only via text later that night that we joke about lunch being our Last Supper.

Whatever the backdrop, we arrive at the art gallery with three hours to explore how the exhibition might stir our thinking about education. The blurb in the book about the exhibition tells us that Culbert was a conceptual artist who used photography and sculpture to ask questions and make people 'look again'.[28] His interest in seeing anew started when his art teacher introduced him to a camera obscura. It is not surprising, then, to find a camera obscura early in the exhibition. The darkened room contains a sphere inside a cube that projects small rays of light like a disco ball. The cube can't control the splash of light on the walls, and what begins as an ordered, right-angled pattern becomes an increasingly random splatter across the room. At the same time, the cube seems to be trying to restore order by drawing the light back in. The rebellious interplay reminds us that nothing is certain or complete.

The spaces between the artworks are like line breaks in a poem. Deliberate and thoughtful, the spacing creates pauses and emphases, as well as offering new meanings in the way the artworks run into each other. We arrive at a section of the exhibition titled 'Slow Light and Loose Arrangements', where there is a large table set up with wine glasses. The installation, called *Small Glass Pouring Light*, has a warm and convivial energy; we are certain we can hear chatter and the clinking of glasses. The effect of the poured light into each glass is clever and the resulting shadow looks like a light bulb. We do a double take to make sure they are glasses and not light bulbs on the table.

Further along there is an old leather suitcase pierced by a fluorescent light tube, which I only later realise is a cheeky nod to travelling at the speed of light. Accompanying the artwork are excerpts from Culbert's thinking in *An Understanding of Light*.[29] One excerpt ends with the statement: 'The shortest distance between two points *is* light.'

I read the italicised and emphatic *is* as the joy that comes with coming to know something that is true for the very first time. The pleasure of discovery and truth all wrapped up in a slanted two-letter word. I love this sentence so much I say it to you several times and then repeat it to Julia, who shares my delight. I want everyone to feel the joy of discovery.

Throughout the rest of the exhibition, Culbert's attention to light is searching – playful and longing. There are coat hooks and what looks like music stands for a group of busking musicians, a vast array of plastic cups for a community picnic and stools that hang upside-down from the ceiling. All are intercepted by light in some way. But what of our quest to distil meaning about education from the artwork? If we lined up Culbert's work side by side and read it like a text, we might say that education should be like line breaks in a poem. Deliberate and thoughtful, education should create pauses and emphases and offer new

---

[28] J. Waite and J. Clemens, *Bill Culbert: Slow Wonder* [exhibition] (Auckland: Auckland Art Gallery, 2021).

[29] J. Culbert, *Bill Culbert: Entre chien et loup* (Paris: Fonds Regional d'art contemporain, 1994).

meanings through the ways ideas run into each other. Education should be convivial and longing, and like being turned upside-down and stabbed with light. Or that education should always involve the joy of discovering something that is true for the very first time. But because nothing is certain or complete, a different configuration – or time of year – would proffer other meanings. The difference between summer light and winter light is everything.

Now Is the Time

My father is reading *New Scientist* and he tells me there is a way to measure the smallest unit of time possible: the present. Given that the present essentially disappears the moment it arrives, this microscopic moment is measured by a Planck length. Light traverses through this length in around 5.4×10^{-44} seconds, making this the shortest time measurable. This explanation is provided in the letters section in response to a reader question about Buddhist meditation and its imperative to live life in the present. The reader asks how long the gap is between the past and the future. One respondent suggests that the present only exists in future memories – that by the time our brains process the present moment, it has already become the past. But I prefer the light-traversing-a-Planck-length explanation best. It seems Bill Culbert was onto something.

Trapping Light in a Jar

When I was a child, the bones in my legs would ache. The dull and distracting throb wasn't growing pains; my bones have continued to ache into adulthood – although not in the same predatory or persistent manner. My concerned parents took me to several doctors, but none of them knew what was wrong. The doctors simply shook their heads in that way that makes you doubt yourself. At the age of five, without any medical answers and to help me deal with the pain, my mother gave me a small jar with a screw top lid. She told me to put the jar on the windowsill so that sunlight would fall in. After a few moments, I was to place the lid on the jar in order to 'trap the light' for later use. '*El rayo de sol*', my mother would say, could be used any time I felt pain. Full of faith in my mother's words, I would trap light and keep the jar nearby like a small arsenal in my war against pain. Whenever the pain started, I would place the jar next to my legs and gently remove its lid. I would close my eyes and imagine rays of light escaping the jar, crossing the barrier of skin and bone, and making its way to the marrow.

Slowly, the icicles I imagined strangling my bones and causing the pain would melt under the medicinal light. My bones would eventually start to glow, free from pain.

Slow Light and Loose Arrangements

I am having an email conversation with a colleague from another university. At first I thought our unexpected talk was accidental, but looking back I realise we both showed up with a need for some shelter. Happening upon each other might have been a coincidence, but our respective need for stillness was a product of inhabiting the same rushing world of academia. After an unexpected meeting, he helped me with an article I was seeking to publish. In between track-changes, something happened. As we neared the final edits, we talked about writing and how we should not get too attached to our words. 'Unless it's a love letter or a manifesto', I said, 'in which case we should chain ourselves to every word'. He wrote back to ask if I offered editing services for such undertakings and then thanked me for bringing a little sunshine into an otherwise rainy, marking-filled afternoon. I decided to confess that I am actually painfully chained to all of my writing and that I live and die with every word. 'Every sentence is a *haka*', I lamented. I think that was the moment our conversation took on new life because the next email from him was about the moon.

Our talk has progressed beyond the article and outside of our university lives – nothing overly personal, mostly lists of what our days involve. We simply report the small parts that make up our lives: a meeting, moderating assignments, food we like, what we are reading or watching. We present this information like a series of dots for the other to join, each newly formed pattern revealing something new. It is a slow undressing. We have baptised our correspondence as our sitting-in-the-sun-time. Holding his day is the easiest thing I do all week. It's as elemental as wanting to know what happens next. I think holding my day is simple for him too: all we have to do is show up and be curious about where the light will fall. On one occasion, he said that he was off to get lunch so he could 'reset his mind' before getting into prepping course materials for next semester. 'It feels as though it never ends', he said, 'prepping/ teaching/marking/prepping/teaching/marking'. I wished him well with the mind reset and said it sounded like a magic trick that only a trained expert could do. But then he explained how going for lunch or sitting down to write to me for a few minutes physically forced him to slow down his thoughts, and consequently his day.

It is a small grace lying down gently next to someone's day. We are all falling a little bit, and if someone comes along and lies down with you so that nobody falls and your day is held respectfully and with care, it is very compelling. We all say 'yes please' because the act is a way of saying 'I see you'. And then we get up and keep going, back to our missions, fighting our dragons and trying not to fall. It's only a moment, but it is no less meaningful, or merciful, or deeply humane. This easy act of a weekly email has become our own slow light and loose arrangement. Our little letters wash over us like light poured from a jar, finding our marrow and making us glow.

I see you, Claudia.
I see you, too.

Albina

My great-great-grandmother Albina outlived two husbands. The first husband was a result of an arranged marriage to an older man when she was a young teenage girl. Eventually, she ran away from him by purchasing a one-way ticket on a boat and travelling to the small port town of Iquique, Chile.

Sheltered between the Pacific Ocean and the Atacama Desert, she met and married my great-great-grandfather Santiago, with whom she had children. For entertainment she would go to boxing matches. Shortly after being widowed, her daughter and son-in-law died, so she took in her four grandchildren and raised them on her own. She did not have much money; beds were shared and meals were modest. As a way of dealing with their material privations, Abuelita Albina instilled rituals into their daily life. After dinner, for example, the family would pass around the youngest of the grandchildren, my Great-Uncle Johnny, and kiss him in lieu of seconds or dessert. If this life is insufficient evidence of her grit, she was equally determined in death. She declared that she would die while out on her daily business so that people would need to come searching for her. Her death happened exactly as she wanted. In her seventies, she collapsed and died in the middle of a dusty street.

I have always wondered about Abuelita Albina's desire to be looked for, but my father thinks her wishes were connected to a certainty that she would be found. That someone would see her and would know who she was and who to contact. Perhaps she played with the idea of being looked for and being found because she knew she would never really be lost. Iquique was a small town where everyone knew everyone – where all familial and social relationships were either known or somehow carried in corporeal form for quick reference.

Nancy Yousef challenges the enlightenment ideal of the self-contained autonomous individual and suggests that Romantic literature presents isolation as an unnatural state.[30] In her analysis of Mary Shelley's *Frankenstein*,[31] she argues that what marks Victor Frankenstein as fully human is his claim to genealogy. While Victor is able to introduce himself by recounting his lineage

---

[30] N. Yousef, *Isolated Cases* (New York: Cornell University Press, 2004).
[31] M. Shelly, *Frankenstein 1818* (Oxford: Oxford University Press, 2001).

(a practice that several characters repeat throughout the novel), the Creature cannot. Indeed, the Creature seems to understand that his desire for 'all the relationships that bind one human being to another' is what stands between him and his humanity. As these relationships are inevitably and devastatingly denied, so too is the Creature's ability to be recognised as human. Yousef's reasoning may help to explain Abuelita Albina's wish that her death should warrant a search party. In this context, the moment of her last breath is not a disappearance or even a final end to existence; instead, it becomes a public marking and setting of relationships. Her family line, her relationships – and consequently her humanity – on display like a thumb print in the sand; inked forever between the Pacific Ocean and the Atacama Desert.

Paying Attention to Where the Light Falls

I am being as slow as light again. Sorry. I am finding my way to your question about how we might make the university more fully human, how we might create more days like the one we had.

If connection and relationships are what mark us as human, then how do we foster these relationships in the context of increased individualism and competition in university life? Perhaps Bill Culbert's commitment to paying attention has something to tell us. The philosophers Simone Weil[32] and Maxine Greene[33] wrote about attention as central to human existence. For Weil, attention is a generosity, which she describes as a type of withdrawal or a standing still. That is, attention is not so much about making the effort to focus but a stopping of movement in order to see what is before us – a means by which to turn away from ourselves and towards the world. For Greene, attention comes from being wide awake and a 'concrete engagement with life'. In which case, perhaps the answer to your question is about paying attention to new things, which are actually old things that we no longer notice. Attention might be the antidote to that gnawing restlessness deep in our chest that there is more than this and better than this.

The importance of bearing witness to the world and to each other suggests that slow wonder *is* educative. Perhaps the role of education is to harness attention so that we can dole it out like a spoon full of sugar or a teaspoon of light.[34] How do we slow down and be still enough to pay attention? How do we trap attention in a jar and carry it around like a big arsenal in our war against the

---

[32] S. Weil, *Waiting for God* (New York: Harper Perennial Modern Classics, 2009).

[33] M. Greene, 'Towards wide-awakeness: An argument for the arts and humanities in education', *Landscapes of Learning* (New York: Teachers College Press, 1978), pp. 161–7.

[34] P. O'Connor, 'A teaspoon of light', *New Zealand Education Gazette*, 90(7) (1980), 5.

fast university? How do we carry our relationships in corporeal form so that we are never fully lost?

We went searching for ideas about education and ended up asking questions about academic life and how we make our university a more humane place to dwell. Given that education is a human endeavour, I don't think we wandered too far from our original intent. Attention. Slowing down. Wonder. Bearing witness. Relationships. These are things I can believe in. Just as I believe in the simplicity of a weekly email exchange as a way of ensuring that I am always found. My pen pal colleague and I live in two different cities, but we have discovered that the shortest distance between two points *is* light.

Peter
Getting and Spending

Dear Claudia,

I've never had someone write into one of my poems before. *Muchas gracias, amiga mia.* When you said you were going to do that, I didn't quite imagine it would look like it does. It gave me such joy. I read it many times. I remember thinking:

> *how your poem lent,*
> *by leaning*
> *into*
> *my poem*
> *an extra layer of grace.*

I read afresh the lines I had written. When I ran them against your words, somehow, they seemed brighter, cleaner, clearer. And then I read your poem down the side of mine, just yours in its entirety. I giggled with the fun and joy of it. Making with words. Yours bent over under the weight of your internal haka, mine bubbling and frothing, tossed in rather than placed delicately on the line.

When you told me you were going to write into my poem, I had feared it might be an intrusive act, transgressive, overly personal. Playing with words on your own is safer than having someone else play with them. You realise how perhaps they weren't so casually tossed after all.

I wondered, as you wrote about light and shade, whether somehow you were colouring in the liminal spaces in my poem. At one point in your letter, you write about the exhibition:

> The spaces between the artworks are like line breaks in a poem. Deliberate and thoughtful, the spacing creates pauses and emphases, as well as offering new meanings in the way the artworks run into each other.

The delicacy of your writing meant you didn't fill in the spaces, you didn't close off meanings but ran the poems together. Our poem became like the exhibition in the gallery: multilayered, incomplete in its completeness, pleasing on the eye and in the ear, a place to meander and revisit with personal and shared meanings. And classrooms could be like art galleries. I think we established that earlier in this book. Or maybe they could become like our poem, a place for playing together to make something never seen before. Imagine if children and teachers played in the spaces in between and made new fresh beautiful things.

Like you, I have taught English at secondary school. I loved teaching Yeats, Dylan Thomas and Keats – especially when it wasn't culturally relevant and I had to work hard to help students find meaning in the words, if not directly to their lives then to the life of the world. But I never once asked them to write inside someone else's poem. I wish I had.

Below I've started a poem. It is rather long so I don't know if we can do another *renga* poem.

The Gates of Eden: Written between Days 80 and 107 in Covid-19 Response Lockdown

I've been
growing my hair long
Even when I'm sleeping
Working for me
Going surfing
Not catching many waves
Lying on my board in the swell
Blowing bubbles with my granddaughter
giggling a lot
We've both been brave on the big slide
Planting out the dahlias
Watering the roses
Writing poems that will never be published
Chatting on the phone to my brother
Idling time
Not working, Covid the perfect excuse
Not wanting to be busy
My quietening city
Watching
Noticing the seasons pass
The sun rising earlier in the morning
The climbing rose outside the kitchen window
keeping time to the seasons
Cooking dinner
Relaxing, knowing
Nothing accomplished again in another day

No irritating stories of Shakespeare
and plagues and King Lear
Spending time imagining
I'm writing this book
I'm half aware
A deadline is
Looming

When I got married, nearly forty years ago, we met with our local priest for marriage classes. We sat and we talked about how we might live together. It was surprisingly instructive, except for the session on sexual relationships, where awkward silence ended eventually with the statement, 'Well, now, You might know more about all that than me.'

Father Sloane, we called him Big Daddy S. He liked the Bible, but he was more importantly a fan of Romantic poetry. So we got on well. He reminded us of Wordsworth's wisdom:

The world is too much with us
Late and soon
Getting and spending
We lay waste our powers
We have given away our hearts.[35]

The endless grind, as Big Daddy S understood, is the consumerist nightmare of having to work to spend, so as to work again.

When I imagine myself as a young man determined not to slip into the hidden machinery, I remain thankful for William and Big Daddy S for reminding me of the emptiness of busyness and business.

They used to teach Wordsworth when I went to school. Now he's not culturally relevant in New Zealand because he is an old white dead man who never saw the Southern Cross and, being English, that makes him an unforgivable imperialist by default. Mind you, we only learnt about daffodils and hosts and none of his thinking about how the Industrial Revolution was killing our attachment as humans with nature. Perhaps if we positioned Wordsworth as a new materialist or post-humanist, he might make a comeback.

We went many years ago to Dove Cottage, and we imagined ourselves rambling with William, STC and the two Sarahs. Someone told us Wordsworth didn't approve of tourists travelling by horse and dray as it was too fast to truly appreciate the beauties of the Lake District. Walking meant you could idle along, rest and lay waste the day rather than your powers.

---

[35] W. Wordsworth & P. J. Rogers (1980). 'The world is too much with us', available at https://bit.ly/3A1zMFM.

William understood that to tarry meant to truly notice the wonder and the beauty of the world that surrounds us.

I despair when I go into some classrooms these days. They are the equivalent of travelling across the Lake District in a space rocket. Full of sound and fury signifying nothing of importance but intensely focused and busy. Learning intentions and goals on whiteboards demanding that every moment of every day is busy. They wrap it in shiny tinsel as preparation for life. Dewey knew: school isn't preparation for life, it is life itself.[36]

There is a deep need built into the capitalist system, which is about creating conditions where we become:

> *Too busy to reflect*
> *Too focused on life ahead to notice deeply the world as it is*
> *Too awake to dream*
> *Too numb to truly feel.*
> *Comfortably numb*
> *Pink might say.*[37]

The Language of Business Overtakes Learning

I sat in my professional year review. Bored. The HR manager told me I needed a career goal. I smiled condescendingly, and perhaps a little assertively, if not aggressively, said

> 'I don't have any career goals or particularly see the point in having any.'
> 'Oh, but you must have career goals.'
> 'Do others have them?'
> She assured me: 'Everyone does. Everyone needs to.'
> 'Perhaps if they didn't mind, I could borrow some of theirs, and then you could say I have some too.'

It was the turn of the HR manager to smile a little condescendingly, or perhaps even aggressively.

Schools are full of goals and plans and forward thinking and are filled to overflowing with crowded curricula, all geared towards individual achievement. Goal-oriented.

> And yet.
> And yet.

I remember that my favourite thing when I was at school, other than the endless hours with my friends being pirates, was the afternoon nap. Sister

---

[36] Dewey, *My Pedagogic Creed.*   [37] Pink Floyd, 'Comfortably Numb', *The Wall* (1979).

Alophonsus, my first teacher, had us all lie down about two o'clock. She must have been exhausted herself by that part of the day, shepherding thirty five-year-olds around a classroom that baked in the summer and froze in the winter. The radio came on and miraculously there were always piano concertos we could listen to, and Sister would encourage us to sleep. No learning intentions, no outcomes except what might come in our dreams. To sleep, to dream perchance, but in that sleep what. . .?

I'll confess I got good at it. Sleeping. Or, more accurately, afternoon napping. In today's education jargon speak, 1 I was achieving napping with merit. There weren't any success criteria, so I can't be sure. I know that, as a lifelong skill, the afternoon nap is possibly the most important thing I learnt at school. That and my impressive ability to replicate piratical swoops, which I practise with my granddaughter when not blowing bubbles.

I'll also confess that when it comes to sleep and dreaming, I have natural talents. As a boy, my favourite song was by the Everly Brothers: 'All I Have to Do Is Dream'[38] became 'jeam, jeam, jeam'. I'd sing it all day when I was four. My special talent was that I could dream while awake. They call it daydreaming. Eyes wide open; asleep but awake; there, but not; in the real world, but not. A sophisticated form of multitasking little appreciated for its delicate and elegant capacity. Sister seemed fine about daydreaming; she understood that it was a liminal space that might bring unexpected rewards.

After Sister Alophonsus and that glorious first year, school days got busier, filled with work. Play was consigned to something we grabbed at between sitting and listening. Daydreaming was considered particularly bad because dreams should only come with eyes closed when we rest, so we can get up again in the morning and go to school and work or, when you're old enough, go to work to work.

It soon became clear to me and my friends that you're supposed to dream just enough to be refreshed, just enough to continue in the dull ache of continuous improvement, of endless personal achievement. No point too in dreaming of pirates without time to be one in pretence with others. For years in class, though, I could feel the dreams coming even with my eyes open and I'd be told to pay attention. I wanted to say, 'I am attending to something far bigger and wonderful than the real world of your maths equation. You tell me I am lost in my own world as if that was a bad thing. I'm imagining whole other worlds that have never been seen by anyone else. I could share them with you, if you only asked.'

---

[38] The Everly Brothers, 'All I Have to Do Is Dream', *All They Had to Do Was Dream* (1959).

Perhaps I might have said, 'Jung describes the process of active imagination in two stages. The first stage is like dreaming with your eyes open. When I'm in my sixties I am going to write a book about the imagination and this is the first step in that process.'

Maybe I could have quoted Virginia Woolf: 'Yet it is in our idleness, in our dreams, that the submerged truth sometimes comes to the top.'[39] I might then have said: 'I'm diving into the silence and peace of dreams searching for truth, even as it surfaces.' That would have scared my maths teachers senseless.

What scared me, when I was young, was that my dad would sing about dreams too, and in one of his favourites he'd sing about being too old to dream.[40] How old, I used to wonder, was too old to dream?

> Did dreams fade slowly or end abruptly for old people?
> And if they were gone, were they gone for good?
> Could I somehow not get too old so I could still dream and not die?

My dad died when he was fifty-one; he never grew too old to dream. Maybe that was a good thing. Dad's song still scares me. But I remember him as he lives in my heart.

I loved the questions Sister Alophonsus asked. They nearly always started the same way, softly, genuinely: 'I wonder. . .'. I would wonder with her too. I still use 'I wonder' as a stem for questions with five-year-olds and PhD students. To wonder, to be full of wonder, and to have the time to wonder. To lie on the floor in class and let the music take you away from the everyday and then slip into sleep. Or gaze out the window, totally inattentive to the drone of the teacher, but paying close attention to my own imaginary worlds.

Schools privilege busywork as much as the world privileges business. Our schools were born at the same time as we built our factories, our dark satanic mills. Schools became places where people as products are stamped out, conforming to the standards set by the factory owners. Now the factory has married itself to the corporate model, stakeholders lurk everywhere and there grows a grinding acceptance that life is purely spent laying waste to our powers in the service of consumerism.

Schools banish idleness and the softness of repose because in these moments we might consider what is unjust and what we might do about it. When schools starve our inner lives, where we are most fully ourselves, we can't figure out who we are, what we believe in and don't believe in, and what we might imagine

---

[39] V. Woolf, 'A room of one's own (1929)', in J. J. Gieseking, W. Mangold, C. Katz, S. Low & S. Saegert (eds), *The People, Place, and Space Reader* (London: Routledge, 2014), 338–42, 339.

[40] The Everly Brothers, 'When I Grow Too Old to Dream', *Both Sides of an Evening* (1961).

we can become. Those who condemn us to lives of getting and spending in pursuit of happiness know that idleness is dangerous – all manner of revolutions can grow in that fallow soil.

In our letters, we've talked about our relationship with the church, and hidden in our words are the confusions of multiple churches, including our own competing versions of the Christian one. Both of us have left, or are in the constant process of leaving and rejoining, that one, recognising you can't do that fully and completely. As I've already written to you, I ended up in the church of the arts and creativity – where did you go?

We both know our educational history well enough to understand that building schooling in the middle of the Industrial Revolution, at a time when the churches were fighting with every fibre of their wealth to control access to knowledge, damned any possibility that education might make genuine change. And you can't help but damn the churches and the Bible back for their delight in work and disdain for rest, for silent repose, reflection and recreation.

Except of course for the Christian God, who was smart enough to work for only six days and then take the rest of eternity off except for another singular day yet to be announced: Judgement Day. The Bible, for us poor non-angelic mortals, condemned us to be ant-like:

> Go to the ant, thou sluggard; consider her ways, and be wise: Which having no guide, overseer, or ruler, Provides her meat in the summer, and gathers her food in the harvest.[41]

Thomas Carlyle, who wasn't shy of flogging off gospels as an apostle of sorts, sold the dignity and the romance of hard work. 'Man was created to work, not to speculate, or feel, or dream', he wrote, adding, 'Every idle moment is treason.'[42] 'Work shall make you free' wasn't just imprinted on the Gates of Eden but has been stamped into our collective consciousness. Bertrand Russell said that the rich 'preach the dignity of labour, while taking care themselves to remain undignified in this respect'.[43] Jeffrey Bernard said the same thing but more acutely: 'As if there was something romantic and glamorous about hard work . . . if there was something romantic about it, the Duke of Westminster would be digging his own fucking garden, wouldn't he?'[44]

I started work when I was fifteen. One of my first jobs was working in a garden for a rich, right-wing member of parliament. Work was then, as it has been all my life, a necessity for food on the table and roof over the head. I'd started work then because my dad was paralysed down the left side of his body

---

[41] Proverbs 6:6–11.   [42] T. Carlyle, *Reminiscences* (New York: Harper & Brothers, 1881).

[43] B. Russell, *In Praise of Idleness* (New York: Unwin, 1935).

[44] T. Hodgkinson, *How to Be Idle: A Loafer's Manifesto* (New York: Harper Perennial, 2007).

and couldn't work. He couldn't even really walk. He shared his dreams and memories with me as I grew up. He sat in his chair. He understood what it was to be idle. It's joy and it's agony.

One day in the garden, the politician's wife stood on the balcony and looked down as I was planting a shrub. She was well-practised at looking down.

> 'Boy, You, boy!'
> 'Yes ma'am?'
> 'That plant. You'll need to redo it. A little more to the left, no, not that far back, to the right. God almighty, is it too much to ask to get it in the right place?'

It was the afternoon after I had sat a national school exam. The politician asked me why I didn't come into work until the afternoon, and I said I had sat my history exam.

He snorted. 'My daughter, must be your age. She did it this morning. Damn political that exam. That's the trouble with schools, damn political.'

I practised my condescending, slightly aggressive smile. I knew even then it would be a useful tool in life.

> 'Yes, history has a tendency to be political', I replied.

In *Walden*, Henry Thoreau summed this all up:

> I sat in my sunny doorway from sunrise till noon, rapt in a reverie, amidst the pines and hickories and sumacs, in undisturbed solitude and stillness, while the birds sang or flitted noiseless through the house [...] I grew in those seasons like corn in the night and they were far better than any work of the hands would have been.[45]

It strikes me as I remember myself as a child and young man that I am approaching retirement. The end of work, a time when again I might find time to do nothing. I'm constantly asked, 'What are you going to do with all the time you will have?' I've been working for just under fifty years. One thing I know is that I ain't gonna work no more. On Maggie's Farm or anywhere else. I'm thinking of making sure I don't grow too old to dream and staying alive to know I'm not that old. I might, like I'm doing in Covid lockdown, keep myself distracted by growing my hair long.

For many of my colleagues at my age, I wonder whether work is about avoiding the inevitability of death and irrelevance. Is it the fear of the wasteland, of returning to our inner worlds that we have studiously avoided by being busy, that forces us to find relevance in another academic article, book chapter, keynote address, successful PhD completion or award? We run faster and faster.

---

[45] H. Thoreau, *Walden* (Boston: Houghton Mifflin, 1964).

We fill our day with the objectives and plans and goals that, since we were five, school taught us make life meaningful. In one recent study of more than 700 people, the majority reported that they found it intolerable to be idle and alone for six to fifteen minutes.[46] I wish Sister Alophonsus had taught them and that she had shown them the wonder of stillness, of listening to the music while lying on the floor.

When I work with initial teacher education students or beginning teachers, it strikes me that they are most nervous about silence in a classroom. They seem to fill it with endless instruction, tasks, endless assessment tasks to make sure the children are tasked to the full. The excuse of a crowded curriculum means they teach quickly, lurching from one measured learning outcome to the next. I model another way of working, of slowing everything down, of not rushing towards predetermined ends but rather of resting in the silence, slowly, joyfully, wondering. So tell me, my friend, about this business of where we start and how we work with teachers learning to become teachers. What of joy, of wonder and surprise? How do we begin to subvert their ways of knowing so they too believe?

Julia Waite
Slow Light and Quiet Reflections – for Claudia and Peter

The way you both describe the pace of university life sounds familiar. Working at a busy art gallery can feel like being on a treadmill of exhibition-making; concepts are pitched, they pass go or not, and if the gates do open the race to the finish can be a gruelling steeplechase. Making *Bill Culbert: Slow Wonder* was full of contrasts: the intensity of realising a complex project coupled with moments of quiet engagement with the artworks and their more intimate legacies. It is only now, with the lights switched off, that I finally have space for slow wonder. This short reflection is an opportunity to consider the last two years working on Culbert in light of your own responses. Let me briefly explain what happened, and what led me to the Centre of Arts and Social Transformation that day in late 2020.

My job with Culbert was to draw audiences into a practice of seeming material paucity and certain conceptual richness. Across nine different spaces at Auckland Art Gallery – Toi o Tāmaki, I built scenes for encounters with different forms of light, framed with the titles, including: *Magic Boxes: Light, Tricks and Illusions*, *Slow Light and Loose Arrangements*, *The Scale of Shadows*, *Levels and Flow*, *Clatter Strike*, *Clouds and Islands* and *Drop and Draw*. The themes were there to guide people into the physical and conceptual dynamism of Culbert's topsy-turvy practice, although quite what they made of the exhibition was difficult to gauge. Unlike at the university, public art galleries have no class role. We have audiences rather than students. Another word for audience is 'visitor', yet most guests who entered the exhibition were anonymous, their presence

---

[46] See https://bit.ly/3oV0U2I.

felt at talks, through feedback forms or via a like on Instagram. Gallery visitors are transient communities with numbers remaining an exhibition's main measure of success – counted by a small metal clicker held in the hand of the attendant.

Right from the start of the project, I was preoccupied with thoughts of the visitor, an interest that echoed Culbert's phenomenology and his own revolutionary reappraisal of art and the role viewers could play in its 'completion'. Culbert believed that aesthetic experience takes precedence over the art object; that the work of art is no longer simply a product of craftsmanship; that the artist is not the only creator of the work. His art stresses the relationship between an object and its environment, which in turn led to my own questioning of the role of exhibition spaces. Culbert stated that he 'was more interested in making brains move than making things or images move',[47] words that became a rally cry and a challenge to try to understand what was at stake in presenting his art – how it would get brains moving. It was no longer acceptable to use art history as the sole prism through which to understand Culbert's work, nor to simply let others responsible for 'audience engagement' develop a visitor programme built solely around talks from experts. Looking back, I see now that my curatorial practice was evolving. The Latin origin of 'curator' is *cura*, meaning to care, which has traditionally been directed towards collections. Working on Culbert was expanding my vision of what care in a public art gallery means, prompting questions about the purpose of art exhibitions and the potential of coming face-to-face with original works of art.

One of the first works to capture my imagination was Culbert's vast *Light Plain*, 1997, an installation that I have only ever looked at on screen. I was drawn to its scale and austerity, and the potential for audiences to stand beneath it and bathe under an illuminated field of electric light. Sadly, capacious *Light Plain* would never fit into the two neat rows of galleries the exhibition was assigned, so I returned to the collection and started to explore earlier artworks, like the specimen of burnt wood pressed beneath a fluorescent tube, *Reefton Cloud*, 1978. While piecing together suites of work from across Culbert's life, I was conscious of being pulled back to the survey, a rather formal exhibition structure designed to assess an artist's entire corpus. Was it necessary to attempt something so comprehensive? I decided early that the exhibition did not need to be exhaustive. I was more interested in recharting some of the main coordinates of Culbert's creative life, plotting them so others could find their way through to a deeper appreciation of the work and its origins. The exhibition would not be a detached consideration of the major phases of Culbert's practice, but rather a series of unfolding chapters, each with its own character, tonality and set of questions.

Alongside the practicalities of making the exhibition, including selecting artworks and fixing and replacing bulbs, was a search to understand Culbert's intellectual life in greater detail. I read the Culbert catalogues, a thesis about his

---

[47] Wedde, I. *Bill Culbert: Making Light Work* (Auckland, Auckland University Press: 2009), p. 329.

relationship with photography, another thesis about the impact of Duchamp on New Zealand art and some Maurice Merlot-Ponty, becoming quickly aware of another narrative drifting beneath the surface. This story was about an adventurous young artist whose imagination and enlivened approach to art were awakened through radical arts education in Aotearoa and Britain. Culbert's exposure to James Coe and Maurice de Sausmarez became not only a history to foreground but a source of inspiration for more fearless and questioning curation. Culbert's experiments with light and perception were causing me to reflect on exhibitions in new ways: what could a Culbert exhibition be about, and what did it have to offer audiences? These fundamental questions about the purpose of exhibitions, and the significance of aesthetic experience, were like currents pushing me in the path of Maxine Greene, and eventually led me to The Centre for Arts and Social Transformation, so aptly shortened to CAST – a space throwing its own unique light.

I came away from our first meeting at the Mt Eden campus with ideas for how the team might approach a visitor programme differently. I also came away with the title. Peter, thank you for giving the project 'slow wonder', which lives on in Auckland Art Gallery's exhibition history, a book, and in my mind as a maxim and eternal provocation. Where do people find slow wonder at the gallery, and what does it look like?

In the context of the gallery, slow wonder might be less about literally slowing visitors down to prolong their dwell-time in front of the art, and more about curators having space to think in an engaged way about the nature of aesthetic experience within their exhibitions. Seeing you both responding to the art in *Bill Culbert: Slow Wonder* on the day before we went into lockdown in 2021 was electrifying. Wandering among the late 1970s magic boxes, your unexpected and at times offbeat responses to the work pinged and harmonised with the incandescent bulbs dotted across the space, stimulating their own small jolts in perception.

Watching you was a reminder of how much individuals can bring to art and to exhibitions if given the space to dream. I wish I had recorded it. We could play the tape back to colleagues to show them what is possible when people can bring their whole selves to a work of art. You were doing what Maxine encourages in her lecture *Blue Guitars: Arts and Aesthetics in Learning* – 'to participate, not simply to contemplate, but to let our energy go out in full encounters with works of art, in transactions that are full of desire'. I felt your desire that day for more time to commune with art freely and more humanely. Maxine was interested in a mode of engagement with the arts and a kind of active participation that makes possible appreciative fulfilment. I interpret appreciative fulfilment as everyone having access to quiet spaces of mystery and wonder. Now, when I think back to the start of the exhibition, I imagine Culbert's small brown suitcase on a railway platform, *Hokitika Return Journey*, 1978. Culbert is beckoning us to grab the luggage, to step forward into lively and engaged aesthetic experiences. Slow wondering can lead to adventures.

Julia Waite
Auckland Art Gallery

4 The Last Supper

Claudia
Against Orthodoxy

~~Start Here~~.

~~Start Here~~.

Start Here.

Amigo, if teaching was a board game or a pinball machine, where would we place those words? I wrestle with this question during a meeting with a group of principals to discuss our new programme. They wrestle with the question too. How could we not? Preparing teachers for the classroom and for a life in education, which are two different things, are serious missions. We comment on the delicate balance between providing a solid practice-base for beginning teachers and opening up a thinking space for all the complexities education imbues. The idea that teaching involves more than learning to teach can be hard to convey to pre-service teachers. As tempting as it might be to say 'education is complex – good luck', we can't absolve ourselves from the responsibility of our work. As we come to this inevitable knot during the meeting, there is a pause in the conversation. We look at each other for the answer, but no answer arrives.

The gap in the conversation reminds me of Paulo Freire's book *Teachers as Cultural Workers: Letters to Those Who Dare Teach*, in which he contemplates what teaching requires of us. He uses words such as emotion, seriousness, affective, joyful, commitment, love and lovingness. The words are all high stakes for Freire, and he makes them ache on the page. I guess that's why he uses the word 'dare' in the title. Your question about *my* church is searching and I like that I have had to push my thinking to give you a response. Well played, my friend. I suppose there are lots of little churches inside the big church of education. And, if I am struggling with the big church, it is worth considering which little one might offer me refuge. The question made me reflect on that meeting with principals and how the question of 'where to start' had led me back to Freire.

It is true, I am sometimes a disciple – I like that Freire never releases us from the broader duty to society that becoming a teacher involves. The argument that teachers should be intellectual and transformative agents in the classroom *and* society is compelling. Freire is not against teacher practice – he values it highly; but he also sees teachers' work as an ongoing process of praxis. Freire defines praxis as critical reflection and action. Through dialogue, he locates praxis in 'the word' because of language's constitutive nature. As we transform the word, we transform the world. I imagine Freire telling us that in the beginning was the word, but the word was not always good. The work of praxis requires a careful balance between critical reflection and action. For Freire, too much reflection leads to inaction, and action without reflection leads to empty activism. In *Teachers as Cultural Workers* he appeals to this delicate balance by asking teachers to develop a patient impatience.

Praxis also involves love, or, as Freire puts it, the courage to love without being branded 'unscientific'. He says:

> The task of the teacher, who is also a learner, is both joyful and rigorous, it demands seriousness and scientific, physical and emotional and affective preparation. Those who commit themselves to teaching develop a certain love, not only of others but also of the very process implied in teaching.[48]

Finally, praxis also requires humility from us, a commitment to not knowing and unknowing through dialogical engagement. We might say that, through praxis, Freire calls for a wider conversation about how we make education good and right. That is to say, questions about how education and society *should* be. Biesta would refer to this wider conversation as a distinction between normative and technical validity,[49] a fundamental difference between the means and the ends of education where the drive for effective practice (the means) eclipses the broader purposes of education. What is teaching and what are the purposes of education are bigger questions that will always inform everything that happens in classrooms, whether we choose to engage with these questions or not.

Freire's vision for teachers is broad, urgent and heavy with responsibility, yet teacher education becomes more and more bound by absolutes. We might call it the scientification of teaching, an entrenched truth-du-jour that teaching can be captured and tamed into a set of rituals called effective teaching. One example is the Master of Evidence-Based Practice offered at an overseas university. There is so much glory and righteousness built into the title that I imagine all other teacher qualifications dim and lacklustre in comparison. Of course, there are better ways to teach and these ways can be knowable, but how do we show pre-service teachers that a life in education requires them to engage with the broader context in which schooling takes place? How do we teach them to distinguish between the gospel of effectiveness and the gospel of what is good and right?

---

[48] P. Freire, D. P. Macedo, D. A. Koike, A. K. Oliveira & A. M. A. Freire, *Teachers as Cultural Workers: Letters to Those Who Dare Teach* (Boulder, CO: Westview Press, 1998).

[49] G. Biesta, 'Good education in an age of measurement: On the need to reconnect with the question of purpose in education', *Educational Assessment, Evaluation and Accountability (Formerly: Journal of Personnel Evaluation in Education)*, 21(1) (2009), 33–46.

'The Power of the Dominant Ideology is Always Domesticating'[50]

Sometime after our meeting with the principals, I am in a very different type of meeting. We are now preparing to have our courses approved by the Teaching Council of Aotearoa New Zealand. The Council has become a powerful entity that governs much of what happens in the teaching profession, including teacher education. As with Freire's focus on the word, the Council actively constitutes what it means to teach in New Zealand through the Code of Responsibility and the Teacher Standards. The Council states that:

> The Code sets out the high standards for ethical behaviour that are expected of every teacher; the Standards describe the expectations of effective teaching practice. *Together they set out what it is and what it means to be a teacher in Aotearoa New Zealand*[51] (my emphasis).

The Standards and the Code mean that in seeking approval for our programmes, we need to make sure that we were 'embedding' the Standards into all of our courses and assessments. The Standards are a mix of behaviourism and ideology; behave like this and think like that. The behaviours and the thinking are not necessarily problematic. The problem is the way the standards simplify rather than complicate teaching as an intellectual task – there seems little to no space for critique or wonder, or any imagined alternative.

Alongside embedding the Standards, we also have to develop 'key tasks' that are aligned to each standard. Our various courses now contain lengthy lists of key tasks that are incorporated into practicum learning outcomes and course assessments. The Council also asks for an assessment that combines a number of the key tasks, which they have unironically titled the Culminating Integrative Assessment, or the CIA, for short. Yet another part of the approval process presents us with an assessment framework that asks us to describe the behaviours associated with the particular outcome or skill we are assessing. The Council's praxis in its relationship to teacher education and the praxis it advocates for teachers seem far removed from Freire's ideas.

When we come to the assessment framework part of the meeting, my colleague and I wrestle with how we describe deep thinking and critical engagement as an observable behaviour. Students in the pose of *The Thinker* by Rodin? As constrained as we are by the Council's process, we engage in an act of policy refusal and rewrite one of the Council's Standards on our course pro-forma. We change the elaboration of the standard from 'design learning that is informed by national policies and priorities' to 'critically examine national

---

[50] Freire et al., *Teachers as Cultural Workers*, p. 10.

[51] Teaching Council of Aotearoa New Zealand, *Our Code and Our Standards*, https://bit.ly/3pqO9NJ, p.ii.

policies and priorities'. We take our battle to the word in the hope of remaking the world.

What is the opposite of behaviourism and ideology? Or, as Freire would put it, domesticating ideology. The day after our meeting with the Council, I visit a student on practicum. I enjoy visiting students while they are on practicum. There is an intimacy about these moments where one is a teacher in the form of gentle observer and commentator. I can't overstate the importance of the gentleness; this exposure will remain an enduring aspect of teaching life.

But these visits come with hooks too. There are practicum reports to be filled with specific outcomes plotted against a range of specific practices. The intimacy of the observation is disrupted by these outcomes so that the experience of learning to teach is diced up into observable and measurable chunks. These outcomes do not just frame the observation in certain ways; they also turn me into a certain type of teacher educator. I am trapped in the Council's version of teaching; behaviourism and ideology weigh heavily in my practicum folder.

During this observation, I become stumped in one part of the report that asks me to comment on the student teacher's capacity to use technology in the classroom, specifically: 'Use digital technologies to foster and enhance collaboration'. I am stumped because I have just witnessed an excellent lesson in which students were guided through a poem by a skilled young teacher without the use of technology. The poem, 'Disabled' by Wilfred Owen, moves between the past and the present to convey the devastation and senselessness of war. The writing is not immediately accessible to students, but, guided by a thoughtful activity and a humming discussion, the students are able to see poet's intent. They are able to grasp the contrast between the touted glory and the brutal reality of war. They are *moved* by Owen's words. I stare at the report and write 'Poetry does not require technology to thrive in a classroom or enhance collaboration'. It feels childish to say so, but I say it anyway because I have no patience with my impatience over the outcomes in the report. All I can see is the contrast between the touted glory and the senseless reality of transplanted outcomes on poetry.

'There Is No True Word That Is Not at the Same Time a Praxis'[52]

A few years ago, our faculty ran a Master of Teaching programme, which I helped to run. The course was small and involved new and creative elements for how we prepared beginning teachers. One of those elements involved working closely with a small group of students at their practicum schools on a weekly basis. These visits to the school involved much more than the

---

[52] Freire, *Pedagogy of the Oppressed*, p. 63.

traditional practicum observation, and they not only allowed us to work closely with our students but also allowed us to develop a relationship with schools. The programme was developed from parameters set by the Ministry of Education, which among other things asked for a focus on working with priority learners. That is, Māori and Pacific students, students from low socio-economic communities, students for whom English is a second language and students with specific learning needs. To maintain a critical focus on the notion of 'priority learners', we ran a course on teaching for social justice and inclusion.

The heating is always breaking down in the building where we met for this particular course, and coats that were taken off were quickly put back on. The building has an old boiler and its perpetual state of breaking-down is a salient reminder of all the things that are broken in education and society. All the more reason to get this course right. I was a little uneasy about teaching a course with the words 'social justice' in the title. Not because I am against the notion, but because social justice is complicated and teaching for social justice is not always straightforward. Nevertheless, beginning a conversation with future teachers was important and my colleague and I thought carefully about how we conveyed the complexities of educational justice.

In one class, we were discussing the attack on public education and the corresponding attack on teacher professionalism. As a provocation, I used a *Time* magazine cover depicting a judge's gavel coming down on an apple. The main title read 'Rotten Apples' followed by a caption that claimed it is almost impossible to fire a bad teacher but that some tech millionaires have the answer to (public) education's problems.

Despite the cold, the coats came back off. I could see the heat in their eyes over this portrayal of teachers and the stinging indignation over tech millionaires who save the day. Throughout the course, there were moments like this, with deep reactions and fire in the belly. The discussion would always flow with little input from me, and it seemed that when we talked like this we were beginning to engage in the kind of praxis that Freire talks about. Developing a patient impatience and a sense of agency in relation to education.

The programme was intense and taught over three semesters, which left only two weeks between each intake. The programme was intense for our students as well, and they always impressed us with their intelligence and commitment to teaching. Despite the workload, we embraced the opportunity to work so closely with students. The family-like feel was a recompense for the relentless machine that is university life. As such, I felt compelled to mark the end of the pro-gramme by writing the class a letter.

There was an intimacy to writing letters, a care I felt for my students even if they didn't feel it for me. I wanted them to know they had my attention, that while I was eating my breakfast cereal, I was conjuring words just for them. The first letter I wrote was called 'Rotten Apples' after the *Time* magazine cover we discussed in class. The letter ended like this:

> I want to leave you with that image because I want you to remember the fight that arose in you that day. Being battle-ready is not a bad thing for teachers. It means you are hungry and, well, a little bit rotten. So, embrace the fight in you and be rotten to injustice. Be rotten to low expectations and low-level classroom content. Be rotten to the eye-rollers and the cynics. Be rotten to everything that stands in the way of making education good and right.
>
> Remember the image and make it your own. Be Rotten Apples of the Radical Sort.

One of my students sent me a text a year later and told me he was still 'keeping it rotten'. At the end of the following year, I found myself wondering what to write – it was the end of the programme but the start of their teaching journey, so, where to start? Which church would I send them to? How would I show them that thinking against the orthodoxy *is* praxis? I typed out Freire's explanation of praxis and wrote to my students:

> Within the word we find two dimensions, reflection and action, in such radical interaction, that if one is sacrificed – even in part – the other immediately suffers. There is no true word that is not at the same time a praxis.[53]

Dear brand-new teachers,

> As you pack your belongings and stride towards the door, I have one task left: to discover what I might have forgotten to tell you. I think I have covered the obvious things, but I might have left out the part about language and how words have more than one side. So listen, here are some words that govern teachers' lives.
>
> *Effective teaching.* These words are often presented like a recipe with steps to follow. The problem is that the steps can become more important than the meal. They end up confusing the means with the ends, so that the means become the ends, and at the end, no one knows what that means.
>
> *Evidence-based practice.* These words are a trap and should be approached with caution. They operate shrewdly by using circular logic, which means they are impossible to refute without sounding like you're against evidence. They are famous for being famous and should be denounced accordingly.
>
> *Accountability and targets.* These words will stalk you. They feed on league tables, and competition and performance indicators, and are always asking for the measuring of this and the ranking of that. Their rabid spit

---

[53] Ibid., p. 63.

poisons everything they touch, so avoid them or you will end up valuing only what you measure instead of measuring what you value.

But remember, when we sat in class that day, we unravelled that teaching can't be reduced to a technical task. And we declared that there is a life and death difference between being an effective teacher and making education good and right. Our labour therefore lies in reimagining and reclaiming these words by turning them over to their other sides.

Effective teaching. Don't get lost in the steps, they are not the end. Being effective is about remaining wide awake and committing to wonder. It means holding the tension and the unknowing with conviction and courage. You should approach teaching with the same delight with which you approached puddles when you were young. It should be a love affair you never recover from. And a puzzle you never learn to solve.

Evidence-based practice. Evidence comes from all sorts of places. Stories are data too. Run your fingers slowly over all of the edges of school life so you don't miss anything. You will find these stories inscribed in hunched shoulders, in hopeful eyes, in shy smiles and in frustrated fists. They will be found in mission statements and policy frameworks. Look for them in the student who doesn't fit in. Look for them in the aspirations of *whānau*[54] you meet. Start a collection of stories. Assemble them thoughtfully, like beautiful works of art.

Accountability and targets. Speak back with the words 'responsibility' and 'solidarity' instead. Become accountable to the marginalised and make their struggle your struggle. Target injustice whenever you see it. Make education a promise you can't break by taking a vow in front of a priest. Or swear it in court in front of a judge. Cross your heart. Set it in stone. Guard it with your life.

It is a true thing, dear brand-new teachers, that all words really do have more than one side. Some sides deliver more of the same. Other sides offer hope; start here.

Peter
Imaginary Worlds

Dear Claudia

I used to write letters to Dorothy Heathcote. When she wrote back, I'd get my original letter back with her thoughts and ideas or imaginings scrawled between and on occasions over the lines I'd written. I was tempted to do that with your latest letter, which seemed to nearly pull this book together. Thank you for resisting that desire. I can almost sense the end, although there might be more to come.

As you were writing about praxis, I wondered if perhaps I should share some of mine. Just this last week I've been working with initial teacher education

---

[54] Whānau = family.

students learning how to teach senior high school drama and dance. We are looking at how to teach 'Billy Goats Gruff'.

'Billy Goats Gruff' is at one level a simple children's story about three goats and a troll who sits under the bridge. His role in the story is to scare goats so that they don't eat all the grass on the other side. At another level, it can operate as an allegory for teaching about terrorism. It requires bravery to teach about that.

One option in drama classes is to act out the story. That approach is to imaginative pedagogy what painting by numbers is to art. A skills-based transactional approach would see children rather meaninglessly practise the movement of goats crossing the bridge and running away from the troll.

Yet I want them to help their students to wonder, what it is like to *be* a troll? To hide in the dark with the job of scaring others? I want to find ways, with their imaginations warm, for them to dig playfully and meaningfully inside the story.

I ask them in small groups to imagine the landing page for an online prospectus for troll school, the place where you learn to scare.

They use their bodies to create the central image and use the idea of a GIF to make it rhythmically move. Bodies crawling, faces contorted to scare, grabbing at goats, eating them, trolls glorying in their victories over the goats. Groans of dying goats and menacing trolls send us into fits of giggles. After all, it is just imagined fun. And we sit together, happy in this crazed Omicron-surging pandemic, joyful at being together in a classroom.

> If we were able to look in troll classrooms, what might we see? Can you show us?
> Troll history classes telling us why goats deserved to die?
> The history of great trolls?
> Goat identification?
> Techniques in scaring?
> Techniques in hiding, in waiting, being prepared to act when needed?
> Goat-cooking classes?

We are leaning into the idea of curriculum as they start dreaming of their first real classes to teach. We are laying the seeds to wonder about how and why we teach what we teach and how that reflects and shapes the world in which we live.

I wonder what things are said on the morning when the baby troll first starts school. Improvised, overheard conversations:

> Make sure you misbehave.
> Learn who we are and why we must defend against the goats.
> You're not the first and you won't be the last. Stiffen up, and off you go.

As we sit after this activity, one of the students talks about how threatened she felt as a young troll with these huge expectations placed on her to live up to what she called 'the legacy of war'.

And when you finish school, your mum and dad write to you a letter. That letter gives advice to you as a new grown-up troll in the world. Underline and memorise the words you think are most important for the troll to remember.

Now we have arrived at the beginning of the story about the Billy Goats Gruff and the troll.

The two chairs at the end of the alleyway represent the bridge. I'll walk down the alley to the bridge. I'll be the troll on my first mission, ready to take my place under the bridge. As I'm creeping down the alley, I can hear the words of my parents (the words you underlined). I'll put this backpack on to signal I am in role.

> Don't be afraid, we are with you.
> Remember who you are and who you come from.
> Remember who you fight for. Never surrender.
> We know you will do your duty.

As I step between the chairs, I pull my bag closer to my chest. My breathing is short and heavy and fills the silence. I screw my face into a grimace. I declare I am determined to do my duty, and in that moment I imagine the Ukraine and young Russian men sent to kill and die for something they were told they must do.

We sit and talk of what we made together, how we had created an imagined world and in doing so had started to question more deeply our lived one. Instead of replaying the story, we had gone inside, under and alongside the story to end as it starts with a killer in hiding. We talked of how this might help young people wonder about who the trolls are, about who determines who gets seen as trolls and who determines who are innocent goats.

Building empathy for the troll is not about being sympathetic to their cause. It is about walking in their shoes long enough to understand their willingness to die to kill us.

The room grows quiet as I suggest 'Billy Goats Gruff' provides a safe place to take the risk to talk about not only things that matter but also things we feel we can't talk about.

Is this praxis close to what we have been talking about in our book? A search for meaning and truth and a wondering about the world. A slow investigation of a story, so slow that our hours of work merely takes us to the start of the story. You asked where we might start, and I find myself saying in classrooms we start and finish in the space in between, between the visible and the invisible, in the heat of the crucible. We start – like Carl Sagan – with the belief that we are made of stardust.[55]

---

[55] C. Sagan, *The Cosmic Connection: An Extraterrestrial Perspective* (New York: Doubleday, 1973).

Claudia
Revelations

Colega,

Our university has embarked on a project to reset and transform the ethos of the place. 'Place' is the key word, because part of the reset is about making our place in *Tāmaki Makaurau, Aotearoa* and *Te Moana Nui a Kiwa*[56] fundamental to how we conduct our work as a university. The Dean has asked whether I will join our faculty's team on this ambitious, and often ambiguous, project. I suspect the invitation to join the taskforce means there are no other hapless takers. However, I have just come back from a conference and I am more self-assured than I should be, so I agree to participate.

The taskforce meetings take place on a different campus from ours, and I am excited to see that we are meeting in the building where I completed my postgraduate studies many years ago. The Fisher Building is where I committed to a relationship with education. Like a first love, I still swoon when I walk the building's corridors. On the first day we meet, colleagues from across the university gather in a room that is too small for the number of people present. The smallness of the space intensifies everything in the room; voices are louder, movement is more disruptive. Worse, the tiny distance between bodies is uncomfortable – a kinship we are not quite ready for. I am worried that I am unable to get into Microsoft Teams and feel generally unprepared for the day ahead. Next to me, a colleague has not only managed to get into Microsoft Teams but has also printed relevant documents and organised them in a ring-binder – with coloured dividers. It is the first day of school and I am already behind.

As the day unfolds, our quest is explained to us. There are things that are written down, official discourse, openly acknowledged and embraced. They are aspirations we wish to paint in bright colours, a certificate to be proudly displayed on our fridge. And then there are the unsaid, unofficial drivers for change. These drivers are based in a fear about relevance. The university is no longer the It Girl we used to be; we are now a T-Rex and the meteor is coming for us.

The mix of both radical project and customer satisfaction feels difficult to negotiate, the Third Way-ish tone grates on my sensibilities. But the direction is already set, and we are told to think big and be bold. There is no choice but to surrender to the ambiguity and to hold the tension as best we can. Still, this talk of place and home captures my imagination. The desire to bring the margins into the centre is compelling and the notion of place stays with me long after our first meeting has ended.

---

[56] Auckland, New Zealand and The Pacific.

The turn to place reminds me of an assignment in which we ask pre-service teachers to take photographs of urban geographies. Students are asked to take images from the surrounding communities of their practicum schools and to think about how difference is written into the landscape. Restaurant signs, multilingual books in a public library, high-rise fences, security cameras, an old but welcoming couch left on a street corner. Each photograph shows how spaces become places. How society reproduces the centre and the margins. I imagine the geographies of the billy goats and the troll in the same way. The dark underbelly of the bridge versus the bright and open paddocks of the billy goats. Winners and losers by virtue of location and imposed identity.

To satisfy my curiosity about notions of place and its relationship to identity, I do some reading. I learn that place is about ascribing meaning to a specific location. That there is a focus on how spaces change over time and how they are actively constituted in particular ways. Importantly, place is connected to the notions of inclusion and exclusion and how it can play a role in disrupting such patterns. How, then, might the university seek to be a more socially just *place* for its community?

I email a senior colleague who is involved in the project and ask about the thinking that informed the focus on place. I smile as I write my email; it has been almost thirty years since Alison taught me in the Fisher Building. She responds and begins by noting the difficulty of thinking about the local when universities are used to thinking about themselves in terms of their international reputations. In this preliminary observation, I realise the project's capacity to speak back to yet another centre. The centre of rankings and competition, and we're-better-than-you-are, and why-can't-you-be-more-like-your-sister. Alison moves on to explain the commitment to place.

> I think it came out of an Indigenisation project that is going on around the whole world at the moment, and that movement is about presence, and local and contextual perspectives for lasting positive change.

She tells me these sorts of ideas are not new in other countries. The challenge for us is to generate new traditions in relation to place by exploring the histories of our places, and to consider the ways in which we are part of those histories.

> It is a direction rather than a destination, and the ideal is for all university members to experience the university as their 'home', somewhat like their own *marae*[57] in which they have a stake and for which they feel enthusiasm, where they can learn things that will change them and change the world as well.

---

[57] Marae = a meeting place or house.

Weighty aspirations. They seem out of reach. Alison tells me that we should aim for small shifts, slowly moving towards a university that benefits everybody, including those who have been underserved in the institution and in our wider communities. Perhaps these imaginary worlds you talk about are like that, Peter. A direction rather than a destination. A place we are moving towards but never quite arrive at, an imaginary world held up against our lived one like a star chart to guide our journey.

As the taskforce grapples with what it means to incorporate place into our practice, the notion of *relationality* begins to form with the same seductive pull as place. The idea emerges during a discussion about teaching and learning, and our desire for these acts to take place in the physical presence of other people. We have been marked by the pandemic and there is nothing desirable about remote classrooms. Despite the commercial imperative to provide customised goods on an on-demand basis, there is no appetite for this version of university among any of my colleagues. Instead, we want a space that prickles with feeling; the alternative feels bereft of breath.

We refer to in-person classes as face-to-face teaching. *Face-to-face teaching* – the words are sometimes spat out as though they are an anachronism in an irrevocably changed world. But during a meeting, we decide the words are rich with possibility. Face-to-face. *Kanohi ki te kanohi.* They invite us to consider what it means to live a life facing each other and facing the world. (I can hear you asking, Peter, why does it have to be face-to-face, why can't it be bodies with bodies?)

Relationality soon becomes a conceptual touchstone, a conceit that holds our vision for how we would like things to be. Our imaginings lead us to explore the full implications of what they may offer. Going beyond the teacher–student relationship, relationality signals a connection and commitment to ideas and to our world. Our role as academics, therefore, is to foster an ongoing dialogue with ideas and the world so that students come to care for them. Dialogue. dialogical relationships. I am facing Freire again as he stares back at me. A pedagogical praxis based on care and attention to the world, rather than ourselves, certainly feels radical for our times.

Aspelin offers a view of relational teaching as an interruption from being solely with ourselves.[58] An interruption from neo-liberal ontologies that position the pursuit of self-interest as the primary purpose of human existence. The instruction at the start of the project was to be bold and go big. Surely there is nothing bigger and bolder than to argue against the current ontologies

---

[58] J. Aspelin, 'Teaching as a way of bonding: A contribution to the relational theory of teaching', *Educational Philosophy and Theory*, 53(6) (2020), 588–96.

and to work towards a new, social ontology through a university education. I will be accused of ideology, but ideology is in everything, and one that is based on the social individual[59] is one I can believe in.

I write letters to students to establish such relationships. Not just between my students and me, but between them and a life in education. I want pre-service teachers to know that education demands a fullness of response, an ache and a longing that never goes away. Education, in this sense, is a place of wonder and transformation. Maggie McLure suggests that wonder is the threshold between knowing and unknowing.[60] She argues it is this liminality that provides an opening into new and previously unimagined possibilities. McLure also says that wonder is relational 'when I feel wonder, I have chosen something that has chosen me'.[61] In which case, we need to pay attention and be open to the wonder that lies in wait for us. From this view, maybe our place is a state of mind in which education lives in a teeming threshold of possibility.

And so here we swim, Peter, bobbing up and down in a conversation that floats from education to university life and back again. The tide pulls us out and the tide brings us back. I suppose education and university life are entangled in each other as we are entangled in them. Perhaps our only recourse is to let everything unravel until only a single thread remains between us and the ideas we make and unmake each day. Dialogical relationships complicate things; they will always result in an unravelling. Dialogical relationships will lead to more questions and further uncertainties. That's the consequence of being open to wonder; we solve the Rubik's cube and then we mess it up again. Our task is to create a place, a home, that is a sturdy enough thread to withstand the complications and the messing up. We need to hold on to this thread so that when the unravelling happens and we decide to leave church, our commitment to and belief in education persists.

We are in an ongoing relationship with education. That is why I tell students that teaching should be a love affair they never forget, or a puzzle they never learn to solve. Education's state of always becoming *is* the end-game. We should be glad for the wrestling because it means we are still engaged. Sometimes all we can do is stand back and look on and trust that the thread will hold. Wonder is the thread that stops us from giving up or surrendering to cynicism. Wonder is the thread that allows us to make and remake education landscapes free from orthodoxy and certainty. Wonder is an

---

[59] J. Dewey, *Democracy and Education* (MacMillan, 1916).
[60] M. McLure, 'The wonder of data', *Critical Methodologies*, 13(4) (2013), 228–32.
[61] Ibid., 229.

ache and belief that provokes us towards imaginary worlds in which we make education good and right.

These imagined and longed-for worlds are our country and this never-ending conversation between us is our place.

Every meal is our Last Supper; we sit at the table and become fat with belief.

Acknowledgements

Our deepest gratitude to Evan and Kath Christian and the AGE Foundation Charitable Trust for their enthusiastic and generous support of this writing project. Our thanks as always to the Chartwell Trust for their ongoing support of our work at the Centre for Arts and Social Transformation, The University of Auckland.

Cambridge Elements ☰

Creativity and Imagination

Anna Abraham
University of Georgia, USA

Anna Abraham, Ph.D. is the E. Paul Torrance Professor at the University of Georgia, USA. Her notable publications include *The Neuroscience of Creativity* (2018, Cambridge University Press) and the edited volume, *The Cambridge Handbook of the Imagination* (2020).

About the Series

Cambridge Elements in Creativity and Imagination publishes original perspectives and insightful reviews of empirical research, methods, theories,or applications in the vast fields of creativity and the imagination. The series is particularly focused on showcasing novel, necessary and neglected perspectives.

Cambridge Elements ≡

Creativity and Imagination

Elements in the Series

A full series listing is available at: www.cambridge.org/ECAI

Printed in the United States
by Baker & Taylor Publisher Services